Off Limits

Off Limits

A PARENT'S GUIDE TO KEEPING KIDS SAFE FROM SEXUAL ABUSE

Sandy K. Wurtele, Ph.D., and Feather Berkower, M.S.W.

Brandon, Vermont

First Edition

Printed in the United States of America

10 9 8 7 6 5 4 3 2

Library of Congress Catalog-in-Publication Data

Wurtele, Sandy K. (Sandy Kay), 1955-

Off limits : a parent's guide to keeping kids safe from sexual abuse / Sandy K. Wurtele and Feather Berkower. -- 1st ed.

p. cm.

Includes bibliographical references and index.

ISBN 978-1-884444-83-8

1. Child sexual abuse--Prevention. 2. Sex crimes--Prevention. 3. Children--Sexual behavior. I. Berkower, Feather. II. Title.

HV6570.W86 2010

362.76'7--dc22

2010029734

P.O. Box 340

Brandon, VT 05733

www.safersociety.org

(802) 247-3132

Safer Society Press is a program of the Safer Society Foundation, a 501(c)3 nonprofit dedicated to the prevention and treatment of sexual abuse. For more information, visit our Web site at www.safersociety.org.

Off Limits: A Parent's Guide to Keeping Kids Safe from Sexual Abuse

$20 plus shipping and handling

Order # WP139

Illustrations: Bert Dodson

CONTENTS

FOREWORD

The night I was crowned Miss America, Burt Parks (the emcee) did something that he had never done before. As I completed my walk down the runway, and the clock was nearing midnight, he said, "The Van Derbur family. Where is the Van Derbur family? Please turn the lights up." Parks scanned the audience of 25,000 people and said, "There they are. Please come on stage. We want everyone to meet the family."

My three beautiful older sisters, my gracious mother, and my handsome, millionaire, socially prominent father walked down a very long aisle and across the stage (the size of three standard basketball courts) as Parks introduced each one. Our family would soon be on the front page of almost every newspaper in America.

Little did anyone know that my father had sexually assaulted me from age 5 to age 18. The world didn't discover the truth until 33 years later, when a newspaper reporter in my hometown of Denver learned that I was an incest survivor. The news was an immediate front-page story. Denver was stunned. Not their Miss America. Not this family.

When I awoke to find "my story" on the front page, I believed my life was over. All the respect and success I had garnered would be for naught. No one would ever look at me the same way again. I felt dirty, bad, ugly, and unlovable—a belief system shared by many rape survivors. My husband, Larry, my college-age daughter, Jennifer, and I locked ourselves behind doors and shuttered windows. Then three days later, my eldest sister's story of incest by our father appeared on the front page, along with my picture. I had pleaded with her the previous day not to come forward. When I stared at the front page of the *Denver Post* that morning, I said to Jennifer and Larry, "I have to get away."

So we went, as we often did, to our neighborhood high school track to jog. A woman who often brought her dogs there—a woman I always said "hello" to—stopped me and said, "We are so proud of what you're doing, Marilyn, and I am so grateful that your sister Gwen came forward this morning." Not feeling grateful, I said, "Really? Why?" The woman replied, "Because yesterday on our most popular radio talk show, people were calling in and saying, 'Why should we believe her?'"

I was stunned. I had been one of Colorado's most successful women. I said, "If people are not going to believe 53-year-old me, then who, dear God, is going to believe a child?" It was a life-changing moment for me. I immediately went home, called our two local newspapers and four television stations, and said, "Here is my home phone number. Today is the first day of the rest of my life."

In the weeks immediately after the stories broke, over 3,000 survivors in Denver came forward for help and support. Research, by the Kempe Center in Denver, with 224 adult survivors found that their average age at the time of their first sexual violation was six. The research also revealed that those who had told a parent before age 18 had encountered the following parental reactions: anger with the child (42 percent); blame of the child (49 percent); refusal to take the disclosure seriously (50 percent); and/or hysteria (30 percent). Some of those young survivors experienced more than one of the listed responses from their parent.

When I disclosed to my mother, she said, "I don't believe you. It's in your fantasy." My mother's response was devastating. I was 48 years old when I told her. Most children and teenagers don't ever tell. Too many adults don't tell, either.

When Michael Reagan was eight, a camp counselor sexually violated him. "By the time I was eight, I hated myself," he reflected later. Michael did not tell anyone until he was 43 years old and his father was president of the United States.

Teri Hatcher, a well-known television actress, was 41 before she could tell anyone that her uncle had sexually violated her as a child. She calls it her "greatest trauma."

Most children don't tell, even when asked. For this (and for many other reasons) our energies urgently need to go into prevention and protection. Child sexual assault is preventable. You are not powerless. You can keep your children safe—through education and through applying the safety tips taught in this book.

Twenty years ago, we didn't worry about abuse being committed against our children by camp counselors or youth leaders or, most disturbingly, family members. Our understanding of the prevalence of such abuse by trusted authority figures has changed significantly since then. In recent years, online sexual predators have also become prevalent. They form a new and very disturbing threat to our young. It is essential that we protect our computer-literate child/teen. Now that we know that one in eight children is sexually violated before the age of 18, it is our responsibility not just to become educated and aware but also to put our collective efforts toward prevention.

Off Limits gives you the information you will need to help keep the children in your life safe. Having an understanding of how sexual abuse happens is the first step in preventing it. And knowing ground rules for your children also can help protect them. For example, do you know how much privacy your child should have? Does your child know what to do if you are separated from him/her in a public place? Are secrets okay? How old should your child be before he/she can spend the night at a friend's home? How do you select a babysitter or caregiver? How important is it to trust your instincts?

Because sexual abuse has often been a silent crime, parents need education so that they can learn who potential violators are and the various ways those violators gain access to children. What are the warning signs of abuse? How could you help your child feel comfortable and safe in disclosing to you? And if a child does disclose, how do you respond? All of these questions will be answered in this important book.

The authors of *Off Limits* have spent their lives educating society about ways to keep children and teenagers safe from sexual abuse. Their wisdom and experience are now available to you in these pages. You will find yourself nodding "yes" over and over as you read the authors' suggestions. You will find yourself saying, "That makes so much sense. That is such good advice!" *Off Limits* is a five-star, must-read book.

—Marilyn Van Derbur
author of *Miss America By Day*

PREFACE

Thank you for reading this book and for joining us in our efforts to prevent children from being sexually abused. As mental health professionals, both of us began our work to prevent sexual abuse by teaching children how to keep themselves safe. Although children learned valuable body-safety skills through our classes, we realized that kids could be even safer if parents were knowledgeable about sexual abusers and were able to discuss body safety with their children at home. So we shifted gears and developed workshops and materials to inform parents and other caring adults about ways they could talk to children and keep them off limits to sexual abusers. This book is our response to requests from parents and other concerned adults for practical information and action steps to keep children safe from the crime of sexual abuse.

Parts of this book may cause readers to feel uncomfortable or unsettled. Reading descriptions of abuse can stir up intense emotions. Readers may even feel the need to block out some of the information in this book. But when adults turn their backs on this crime—because it is too uncomfortable to face—children, all too often, are the ones who pay the price. In the time it takes an adult to read through this book, many thousands of children's lives will be changed by sexual abuse. As authors, we promise to help you move from discomfort to action.

As psychologist R. H. Starr said, "To expect to eliminate [childhood sexual abuse] in the foreseeable future is overly optimistic; not to try to eliminate it is irresponsible and indefensibly callous." Children deserve to grow up free from sexual abuse. Together, we can make that happen.

Many people contributed to the making of this book. We are deeply indebted to the hundreds of survivors who generously shared their personal experiences with us. They taught us about trauma, betrayal, resilience, and hope, and their stories inspired us to write this book. We are also profoundly grateful to all the children, parents, and professionals who participated in our educational programs and workshops. Thank you for responding so positively to our messages and for encouraging us to put them into print. We are indebted to the many authors, researchers, and clinicians cited throughout the book for enriching our understanding of this crime against children. To our many friends and colleagues, thank you for your invaluable suggestions, gentle criticisms, and unyielding support. Special thanks go to Lisa Decker, Annie Gardiner, and Maureen Kenny. Thanks to our attorneys—Michael Berger and Lisa Lucas—for helping us to get the manuscript into publication. We also express heartfelt appreciation to our family members for their steady patience and encouragement, which helped us to complete this project.

Two editors deserve special mention—Margaret Sallinger and Marjorie Ryerson. Margaret provided us with brilliant guidance in the book's early development. We appreciated her creative suggestions for structuring the manuscript and for helping us focus on the book's mission. Marjorie, our editor at Safer Society Press, provided continuous support and an unwavering commitment to get this book into the hands of parents and professionals. And lastly, we want to thank Safer Society Foundation members for their dedication to eliminating childhood sexual abuse, and for including *Off Limits* among the foundation's impressive list of publications.

—Sandy Wurtele and Feather Berkower

INTRODUCTION

It seems like sexual abusers are everywhere—in churches, schools, youth organizations, and homes and on the Internet. Hardly a day goes by that we don't read, hear, or watch some news report about children being sexually abused. Driving to work you hear on the news that the husband of a home day-care provider has been charged with sexually abusing the children in his wife's care. Then you read a news story about a schoolteacher accused of molesting students. Later that night on television, you watch an exposé about "cyber predators" who use the Internet to prey on unsuspecting teenagers. This seemingly endless barrage of news accounts may lead you to believe it's inevitable that children will be sexually abused, or may make you feel powerless to protect children from sexual abusers. But childhood sexual abuse is not inevitable and you are not powerless. As you will learn in the following pages, caring adults can do many things to protect children from sexual abuse. *Off Limits* will help educate you about childhood sexual abuse, offer practical action steps for protecting children, and suggest ways to teach children to protect themselves.

Our goal is to help you keep children safe from sexual abusers. The first step is to become educated about the nature of this crime. By the time you've finished reading the book, we hope you will have a better understanding of

- what child sexual abuse is;
- who sexually abuses children;
- how to recognize warning signs that someone may be sexually abusing a child;
- how and where abusers gain sexual access to children;
- how abusers keep their victims quiet;
- how to help a child who has been sexually abused;

- how to help a child who is abusing other children; and, most importantly,
- how to keep children safe from sexual abusers.

When it comes to childhood sexual abuse, ignorance can be very dangerous, but knowledge gives you power and strength. As the English statesman Disraeli once told Queen Victoria, "The one with the most knowledge has the greatest advantage." Disraeli's reasoning applies directly to the subject of childhood sexual abuse. Smarter adults mean safer children.

How to Raise Kids and Teens Who Are Off Limits

As a safety-conscious parent, you're probably already doing many things to keep your children safe from danger in today's world. Maybe you've enrolled your child in karate, judo, or some other self-defense class. Perhaps you drive your children to school instead of allowing them to walk or ride their bikes. Maybe you've installed a nanny cam or had your child fingerprinted. But what can you do to prevent or at least reduce the risk of your child being sexually abused?

Our goal for *Off Limits* is that it will explain childhood sexual abuse as well as provide a prevention tool kit for keeping children safe from abuse. We have structured the book around 32 safety tips, which are based on our clinical experience and research, as well as on insight from other experts in the field of childhood sexual abuse. We also include some suggested language for communicating in a nonthreatening way with children and with those who care for children. When equipped with the information and tools in this book, you can readily apply what you have learned in this book to your own family, as well as to your children's schools, youth organizations, sports teams, communities of faith, and other groups to which they belong.

The practical action steps we offer include the following:

- Teach children body-safety rules within the context of sexuality education.
- Screen children's companions and activities.
- Create safe environments to reduce the risk that children will be abused.

At the end of the book we also include three handouts: "I Am an Off Limits Kid!," "We Have an Off Limits Home!," and "We Live in an Off Limits Community!" The handouts summarize key points from the book.

Although this book is written primarily for parents (including foster parents, adoptive parents, stepparents, grandparents, and guardians), any concerned adult will benefit from reading *Off Limits*. Extended family members, teachers, child-care providers, faith leaders, youth group leaders, and health-care professionals can all use the safety tips in their respective roles with children. The safety and well-being of children and teenagers are not just parents' responsibilities, but everyone's responsibility. All adults play vital roles in preventing childhood sexual abuse.

Our vision is to live in a world in which children are never seduced, manipulated, or tricked into sexual activities, a world where children's relationships with others are safe, honest, respectful, and supportive, and where their trust in others is never betrayed.

—

There is no trust more sacred than the one the world holds with children. There is no duty more important than ensuring that their rights are respected, that their welfare is protected, that their lives are free from fear and want and that they grow up in peace.[1]

—Kofi Annan,
former Secretary General
of the United Nations

Chapter 1

PORTRAITS OF SURVIVORS

In this chapter, we present the portraits of four children—Sasha, Gustavo, Laura, and Monique. Each represents a composite of sexual abuse survivors we have known, either personally or professionally. We use these four cases to illustrate how and where children are sexually abused—two of them in their own homes; the other two in the homes of their abusers. We will also provide descriptions of the four children's abusers and describe how abusive experiences can affect children throughout their lives. We use these and other case examples throughout the book, but we do not use real names, so that we protect the privacy of actual survivors.

Just as is true with many real children, our four case-study children all participated in sports and other extracurricular school activities, had successes and challenges in school, became close friends with some peers, got picked on by others, and experienced births, deaths, and divorces in their families. We'll revisit these four children in the epilogue and consider ways their abuse could have been prevented by applying knowledge and safety tips from this book.

First, let's meet Sasha.

SASHA

Shortly after her divorce, Maria got a job as a waitress at a trendy restaurant to support herself and her seven-year-old daughter, Sasha. Mike, the restaurant's manager, took a special interest in Maria. During quiet moments in the restaurant, the two of them would talk about the restaurant business, and Maria would share with Mike her passion for cooking and her dream of one day owning her own catering business. After a few weeks, they began seeing each other outside of work. Sometimes Maria and Sasha met Mike at the park or zoo. More often, he came over to her apartment and Maria cooked dinner for the three of them.

Theirs was a whirlwind romance. After a brief but passionate courtship, Mike asked Maria to marry him. Without hesitation, she said, "Yes," and Maria and Sasha welcomed Mike into their family. Maria was thrilled. Not only was Mike someone who loved her, but he also seemed to care a great deal for her daughter. Sasha was thrilled because not only did she like Mike, but also she was glad to see her mom happy.

Once Maria and Mike were married, Maria was able to pursue her cooking passion, something she hadn't been able to do as a single mother. She enrolled in night classes at the local culinary school, and Mike took care of Sasha during those evenings. Feeling comfortable with Mike's interactions with her daughter and with the closeness in their relationship, Maria was more than willing to have Mike care for Sasha. It seemed as if he had always been a father. Mike would give Sasha piggyback rides around the house and tickle her as she giggled with joy. Sasha loved all the attention.

With her talent for cooking and her keen business skills, Maria quickly developed a booming specialty food and catering business. A few years into the marriage, however, Mike lost his job. By now, Maria's business was so successful that she was able to be the sole provider for the family. Mike then became the primary caregiver for Sasha, since he was out of work and Maria's business called her away from home many nights and weekends.

Although he didn't share his feelings with Maria, Mike felt pretty lousy about losing his job and about having to rely on his wife to be the breadwinner for the family. In addition, Mike began to resent that Maria was leaving her daughter alone with him so that she could pursue her own interests. He began to feel unimportant to and neglected by Maria as she immersed herself in her new business. With Maria gone a great deal of the time, Mike began to develop deep feelings of loneliness and bitterness, and his self-confidence deteriorated. During that time, Mike stopped communicating much with friends and other family members, and he became increasingly isolated. Feeling stuck and powerless, Mike plunged to an emotional low. Thank goodness for Sasha, he kept thinking. Always an affectionate, loving child, Sasha adored her stepfather. In those dark years for Mike, a close bond developed between the two of them.

They constantly played together, snuggling on the couch as they watched TV. They cuddled in bed while Mike read Sasha bedtime stories, gave each other back rubs and massages, and bathed together. With her mother gone so much, Sasha thrived on Mike's attention, love, and physical affection.

As Sasha got older, Mike began noticing that she was developing breasts and curves. He found himself becoming aroused by these changes in her body. Slowly, Mike's affection for Sasha turned sexual. Touches that had always been nurturing now became sexual. When they showered together, he began spending more time washing her breasts and genitals. Then he started asking Sasha to "help wash Daddy." During massages, he started "accidentally" touching her genitals. When Sasha didn't object, he began intentionally fondling her. By the time Sasha was 11 years old, the two of them were having intercourse.

Mike was unable to separate the emotional closeness that he felt for Sasha from his sexual feelings. Mike needed so desperately to be loved that he had turned to the one person he believed loved him the most—Sasha—and combined emotional intimacy with sex during a critical time in Sasha's development. Mike told Sasha he was having sex with her to show how much he loved her and how special she was to him. Mike also confided in Sasha about his sexless marriage with Maria. By "loving" Sasha, he convinced himself that he was meeting his sexual needs without having to go outside the family. Sasha trusted Mike and complied with his requests. She feared what would happen if she told her mom what Mike was doing to her, and she also loved Mike. He was like the father she had always wanted. Sasha was afraid that if she told her mother about what was going on with Mike, then she might have to go to a foster home, or her mom would make Mike leave, and their family would fall apart.

Sasha was acutely aware of her parents' deteriorating marriage. She did not want to add any more stress to their already turbulent home life. She attempted to be "perfect" at school, so she wouldn't call attention to what was going on behind closed doors. Sasha's teachers all noticed her perfectionism. She was so obsessed with being perfect that if she made a mistake or got less than 100 percent correct on her tests, she would become very anxious and begin to cry. Through her sobs and tears, she would promise her teachers that she would do better next time. Although they tried, her teachers couldn't reassure Sasha that it was okay to make mistakes.

As the sexual activity between Sasha and Mike intensified and as Mike's feelings for Sasha became more and more compromised, Mike began to consciously isolate Sasha from her friends. Sasha spent almost all of her free time with Mike. Mike would frequently encourage Maria to accept catering jobs, so that he and Sasha could go out on "dates." (Sasha came to realize that when Mike called it a date, it meant they would be having sex.) Although she was confused and sometimes scared by the sexual activity, she also felt safe, loved, and needed by Mike. All of this behind-the-scenes complexity resulted in a depressed young girl who presented herself to the world as a perfect student and daughter. Even when her pediatrician treated Sasha for repeated urinary tract infections, she maintained the perfect image and kept the secret.

When Sasha was 12, she attended a sexual abuse seminar at school and realized that what her stepfather was doing to her was wrong. She couldn't keep the secret any longer, and she told her best friend, whose mom then called Social Services. Social Services interviewed first Sasha, and then Maria, at Sasha's school. When Maria learned that Mike was sexually abusing Sasha, she believed and supported her daughter throughout the investigation and sentencing.

GUSTAVO

After her husband's death five years earlier, Rosie started working full time to support herself and her two sons, Gustavo and Jorge, ages 11 and 7. Even with Rosie's full-time work schedule, she managed to keep up with basic parenting duties of cooking meals and doing laundry, but she often found that she couldn't always provide the emotional support her young boys needed, because of her own emotional despair from the loss of her husband. Rarely did she have the time or energy to do anything with her sons other than homework or meals, even though Gustavo constantly asked her to take him places and play with him like his father had. The family regularly attended church together, which Gustavo loved doing. After his father's death, Gustavo had found himself increasingly drawn to religious teachings, from which he gained comfort and a sense of belonging.

Rosie decided to enroll Gustavo in the church's preteen program, thinking it would give him a chance to further develop his religious interests and the opportunity to make close friendships and have some fun. Because Gustavo was physically small for his age, his classmates often teased him at school. They also taunted him with painful racist comments. School personnel frequently overheard him saying disparaging things about himself, especially about his abilities to do "masculine" things like the bigger boys did.

In addition to making new friends in a culturally diverse setting, Rosie hoped that the youth program would provide Gustavo with the much-needed attention of a grown man. Kevin, the youth pastor, a 30-year-old polite, intelligent, and caring man, had an excellent reputation among the other parents as not only a good role model but also a strong mentor, capable of boosting a boy's self-esteem. The other boys in the group adored Kevin, as did Gustavo. Kevin soon began showing Gustavo the love and attention the child had longed for. A close bond developed between the two.

Over the course of the next three years, Kevin emotionally and sexually abused Gustavo on a regular basis. Although Gustavo's self-esteem initially improved when Kevin first took him under his wing, it plummeted once the relationship became sexualized. Gustavo acted out his trauma in many ways. His self-doubt was evident in his schoolwork (failing grades) and in his behavior during class. He constantly got in trouble during class time. He had a difficult time sitting still and concentrating and would fidget and pester his classmates. His teacher referred him to the school counselor, who suggested that Gustavo be evaluated for possible attention deficit disorder. Rosie took Gustavo to the family pediatrician, who prescribed medication for his hyperactivity. Although the medication helped Gustavo focus on his schoolwork, it did nothing to help him with his peer relationships, which had worsened. Gustavo started expressing his anger through aggression, and he received several suspensions for fighting. Then he began to act out his anger and rage by sexually abusing his younger brother. As he acted out in more and more inappropriate ways, Gustavo's cries for help went unheard. Only after Kevin was transferred to another church in a different city did the abuse stop.

LAURA

Laura, age 10, lived with her parents and her two siblings—brother Chris, 14, and sister Lynnette, 7. To the outside world, theirs looked like a normal, well-functioning home, with working parents and three nice kids. But on the inside, certain features made it a high-risk home for sibling sexual abuse. First, sexuality was not discussed. When the children had questions about their bodies and sexual development, their specific questions were left largely unanswered, and "such talk" was discouraged. When Chris became curious about sex, he didn't feel he could talk about the topic with his parents or even with other teens. Second, although Chris was physically large for his age, he was immature socially and frequently rejected by his peers. He spent most of his spare time hanging around the house bullying and tormenting his sisters. Third, he was disrespectful of the girls' privacy and would frequently barge in on his sisters while they were showering, using the toilet, or dressing. Although both Laura and Lynnette complained about his behavior to their parents, who asked Chris to stop, he didn't. Fourth, he spent long unsupervised hours surfing the Internet.

Both parents were busy professionals. Dad owned a bookstore and Mom was a real estate agent. They both worked long hours and would leave Chris in charge of the two girls after school. During this unsupervised time, he turned to the Internet to get his questions about sex answered. He first frequented porn sites showing people engaging in oral sex. Then he started forcing Laura to do some of the same sexual acts to him. Laura later disclosed, "He forced me to watch that disgusting stuff and then made me do it to him."

Shortly after Chris began abusing her, Laura started refusing to eat dinner with her family. She became very moody and sullen and chose mostly to stay alone in her room. Once there, she began cutting on her arms and legs with razors, but she always covered up the marks so that no one could see them. Laura often complained about how much she hated her older brother, but her parents dismissed her complaints as nothing more than sibling rivalry. Chris's abuse of his sister lasted for four years and stopped only when he left home for college.

Once she entered high school, Laura became promiscuous and started dating much older guys. Her schoolwork suffered because of all the emotional stress she was under. She often skipped school, and any attempt by her parents or teachers to address her failing grades was met by increased rebellion. She finally confessed to her mother that she was skipping school to "hook up" with her boyfriends. At that point, her mother immediately set up an appointment at the school health clinic for Laura to get on birth control pills. She managed to graduate from high school but left for college with her emotional problems in tow. When she was on the verge of flunking out of college, she disclosed her brother's abuse to a campus counselor, who then helped her to begin her healing journey.

MONIQUE

Monique ("Mo") lived with her mother Wendy and father Bill until she was 11 years old, at which point her parents got divorced. A year later, her mother married Steve. Mo had a very difficult time with her parents' divorce, and she blamed her mother for "ruining her life" by leaving her father. Mo resented her stepfather, especially for the way he tried to control her and be her substitute father. In addition, Mo had just entered junior high, and she felt lost in the big school where seventh graders were the underdogs. Mo was supported during this trying time by her homeroom teacher, Miss Jenkins, who took a special interest in Mo. They often spent time talking together about her parents' divorce. Miss Jenkins was also the girls' volleyball coach, and she invited Mo to join the team.

Miss Jenkins coached Mo in volleyball from grades seven to nine. In addition to being Mo's teacher and coach, Miss Jenkins also began to assume the role of confidante for the child. Mo felt comfortable sharing her feelings with Miss Jenkins. Mo would tell Miss Jenkins how angry she was at her mother for divorcing her father, how she felt unloved by her parents and misunderstood by her friends, and how she didn't feel she belonged in her family or at school. Miss Jenkins treated Mo more like her equal than a student, and it made Mo feel special. Miss Jenkins asked Mo to call her Judy or "JJ" and seemed to get upset when Mo called her Miss Jenkins. The teacher began inviting Mo to spend nights and sometimes weekends with her. Mo valued the friendship and enjoyed the special attention from this respected and well-liked teacher. She had always been a shy girl, and when their friendship deepened, Mo withdrew even further from her peers. She turned down the few invitations she did get from friends to hang out and instead spent most of her time with Miss Jenkins. Mo's parents were pleased to have such a popular teacher take an interest in their daughter. They appreciated that Miss Jenkins encouraged Mo's athletic talent, and they noticed that Mo seemed less angry at home.

Over time, Mo's friendship with Miss Jenkins grew into what, to Mo, felt like "love," and it was at that point that Miss Jenkins began sexually abusing the young teen. She would tell Mo how much she loved and needed her. Mo believed she could not tell anyone what was happening because of the power Miss Jenkins had over her as her teacher and coach. Plus Mo truly loved Miss

Jenkins, even though the sexual things that Miss Jenkins was doing upset her. As the abuse continued, Mo lost all interest in schoolwork and her grades plummeted. She emotionally withdrew from her parents and discounted any encouragement they offered her about her athletic talent. Mo came to resent her parents for not knowing what was really going on between her and Miss Jenkins. She couldn't understand why her parents continued to praise her coach for Mo's accomplishments on the volleyball court. Once passionate about and excited by sports, Mo was suddenly depressed most of the time. Her depression was evident to family and teachers.

Mo's relationship with Miss Jenkins ended when Mo's family moved to another state at the end of her junior year. Mo did not join the high school volleyball team in her new school.

These composite cases illustrate four children who were sexually abused before they graduated from high school. In all four cases, older, more knowledgeable, and powerful people exploited their authority and used these children to satisfy their sexual or emotional needs.

Childhood sexual abuse happens when a person forces, coerces, persuades, threatens, or tricks a child into sexual activities. Abusers can be adults or minors. When a legal or blood relationship exists between the abuser and the child, it's called incest. Incest is what happened when Sasha was abused by her stepfather (known as paternal incest), and when Chris forced his sister Laura into sexual acts (known as sibling incest). Sexual abuse—whether committed by adults or older children—involves the exploitation of children's naïveté, trust, and innocence.

Childhood sexual abuse often involves physical contact. Some children are "fondled," meaning their abuser intentionally touches their genitals (penis or vulva), anus, groin, breast, or buttocks with an object, hand, or body part. Other children, like Laura, are forced to touch the abuser's genitals. Some children, like Gustavo and Sasha, experience the most severe form of contact abuse: penetration of either the anus or vagina. Sexual abuse can also happen without physical contact. Using a child to film, photograph, or model pornography is considered non-contact sexual abuse. Using the Internet to entice a child (under the age of 18) to engage in a sexual act is also a type of non-contact sexual abuse. Exposing one's genitals to a child, masturbating in front of a child, making a child strip naked or masturbate, or showing images of sexual activity to a child are other examples of non-touching sexual abuse offenses.

The sexual abuse of children is a crime in all 50 states. Many people are startled when they learn how many children are sexually abused. In the United States, one in four girls and one in twelve boys are sexually abused before the age of 18.[1] These figures translate into one in eight children. Given how often children are sexually abused, there is a very strong likelihood that many of our readers are survivors. We acknowledge the unique challenge you may face reading this book and appreciate your willingness and courage to prevent children—your own and others'—from being sexually exploited.

Childhood sexual abuse can be emotionally, physically, and psychologically damaging. Children are confused, hurt, and sometimes devastated by these sexual acts—with potentially lifelong repercussions that may manifest in depression, shame, and problems with intimacy and trust. Long-lasting harm, however, is not inevitable, and about 40 percent of sexually abused children show no signs of psychological damage at the time of their initial evaluation.[2] How sexual abuse affects a particular child depends on many things—the child's personality, the abuser's relationship to the child, how old the child is when the abuse starts, how long the abuse lasts, the invasiveness of the abuse (from fondling to penetration), whether the abuser uses force or violence, how others react to the child's disclosure (if the child ever tells), and whether the child receives counseling.

Given all these variables, it is difficult to predict exactly how a child will be affected by sexual abuse. For some survivors, the abuse leaves scars that never heal. For others, the emotional wounds lessen over time. Sexual abuse survivors are everywhere. Some are healing quietly, while others are healing by speaking out publicly, advocating for other survivors, and protecting children from sexual harm. Perhaps you recognize some of these more notable survivors of childhood sexual abuse:

•

> Former Miss America and incest survivor Marilyn Van Derbur, whom you met in the foreword, educates judges, doctors, nurses, lawyers, teachers, therapists, and parents around the country about the trauma of childhood sexual abuse.

•

Frank Fitzpatrick, a survivor of clergy sexual abuse, formed a national support group called Survivor Connections to help other victims of clergy abuse.

•

Barbara Blaine, also a victim of clergy abuse, helped to establish SNAP, the Survivors Network of those Abused by Priests.

•

Fran Henry, another survivor of sexual abuse, founded Stop It Now!—a national nonprofit organization that among other things works to provide help for abusers, educate adults about ways to stop sexual abuse, and increase public awareness about the trauma of childhood sexual abuse.

•

Talk show host Oprah Winfrey, also a survivor of childhood sexual abuse, educates the public about childhood sexual abuse through programs on her Oprah TV show and Web site.

•

Alicia Kozakiewicz, who at age 13 was kidnapped and tortured by a man she met on the Internet, tells her harrowing story to elementary and middle school students around the country, warning them about online sexual predators.

•

Margaret Hoelzer, U.S. swimmer and 2008 Olympic silver medalist, publicly revealed in a 2008 *USA Today* interview[3] that a playmate's father sexually abused her as a child. She has joined forces with the National Children's Advocacy Center to raise awareness about sexual abuse.

•

These survivors, along with countless others, are heroes for children. They have committed their professional and personal lives to ending the sexual violation of children. They are speaking out, telling their own stories, giving hope to others, and, most importantly, taking a stand against this most reprehensible of crimes against children. Each of us can be some child's hero. You don't have to have special powers, be famous or rich, or even be a parent to take an active role in preventing childhood sexual abuse. Any caring person can speak up for a child who can't say "Stop!" and can intervene when that child's safety is jeopardized. What it takes is the willingness to learn about sexual abusers, the courage to speak up for children, and the commitment to take action.

—

Never think that a few caring people can't change the world,
for indeed, that's all who ever have.[4]

—Margaret Mead, anthropologist
from *The World Ahead:*
An Anthropologist Anticipates the Future

Chapter 2

LEARNING ABOUT SEXUAL ABUSERS

I was about twenty-eight or twenty-nine... and it was weird. I was playing around with [my daughter]. I was tickling her... And I just started tickling her in the wrong places. I thought she liked it. At first... I enjoyed it, but at the same time, I felt real bad about it too. Like, "I can't believe I'm doing this to my own daughter. What kind of father am I?" But... it was probably a month later or so, I did it again. I had convinced myself that she liked this. I'd keep telling myself, "I'll never do that again..." But I did.[1]

—Leon, a sexual abuser, from
Unspeakable Acts by Douglas Pryor

The above quote—from one of the 30 sexual abusers interviewed by Douglas Pryor for his book, *Unspeakable Acts*—is disturbing, to say the least. The image of a person molesting a child can stir up intense emotions, and sometimes those feelings can stand in the way of learning more about abusers. But knowing how and where abusers gain sexual access to children and how they keep their victims quiet forms the foundation for all of our safety tips designed to keep children safe.

Who Abuses Children? The Facts about Abusers

Many people assume that abusers are evil perverts, weird-looking strangers, or creepy-looking middle-aged men lurking at playgrounds. Why do we imagine them this way? One reason is because we simply don't know the facts about people who sexually abuse children. Also, we tend to be swayed by the media, which covers the more sensational cases, especially the very rare and chilling rapes and murders of young children by strangers. Parents desperately want to believe that abusers look weird or stand out in some way so they can keep their children away from them. It's also very difficult for any of us to imagine that someone we love or respect could be a sexual abuser. Parents seem to feel safer believing that strangers pose a greater risk to their children than those they trust and love. The following case illustrates this point:

> *The teachers at Karen's preschool noticed signs that made them wonder if she was being sexually abused. Usually a very outgoing four-year-old, Karen now seemed preoccupied and clingy and appeared reluctant to go home at the end of the day. One day, when the children were drawing pictures of themselves, she drew a penis on her self-portrait. She had also begun masturbating excessively and would often leave fun activities to go rub her genitals. When the teachers expressed their concerns to Karen's mother, she said, "There's no way my daughter could be a victim of sexual abuse, because I don't allow her to be around strangers." Karen was being sexually abused, not by a stranger, but by her grandfather.*

This mother's misinformation that abusers are only strangers kept the mother from protecting her daughter. When parents are uninformed about child sexual abusers, or believe that "sexual abuse doesn't happen in my family or my neighborhood," they can unknowingly put their children at risk.

© Cam Cardow, The Ottawa Citizen and PoliticalCartoons.com

OFF LIMITS SAFETY TIP #1:

Know the facts about sexual abusers.

Recognizing the myths and the facts about people who sexually abuse children can help decrease a child's vulnerability to abuse.

Myth #1: Sexual abusers are most often strangers.

Fact: In nine out of ten cases, an abuser is actually a friend, family member, or authority figure—basically, someone the child knows and trusts. Within families, children (especially girls) are most often sexually abused by parents or parent figures (for example, a mother's boyfriend), but also by siblings, aunts, uncles, cousins, and grandparents.

Strangers make up a very small percentage (less than 10 percent) of abusers. The men who abducted and sexually abused Shawn Horbeck in Missouri and murdered Polly Klaas in California were strangers to those children. Fortunately, these atrocious sexual assaults by strangers are rare. Strangers do not have access to kids in the same way that friends or family members do. Looking back to chapter 1 at the examples of the four children, the abusers were a sibling, a stepfather, a teacher/coach, and a trusted church youth leader. All of the children knew, respected, or loved their abusers.

Bottom line: Children will not be protected from sexual abuse by being told to stay away from strangers.

Myth #2: Only males sexually abuse children.

Fact: Most, but not all, abusers are male. Nationally, the U.S. Department of Justice reports that females account for less than 10 percent of all adults and juveniles who are arrested for sex crimes. However, the report also points out that females are less likely to be caught and prosecuted.[2] Why might so few cases of female-perpetrated sexual abuse be reported to the authorities? One reason is that women can mask some forms of abuse under the guise of care giving (for example, while bathing, dressing, or sleeping with children). Another reason is that sexual relations between adult women and teenage males are often glorified or depicted as coming-of-age rituals rather than abuse.

Because of this double standard, boys may be less likely to report when they have had sexual contact with women.

When female abusers are caught, they often fall into one of the following groups:

- Women, generally in their 30s, who are under the misperception that they are in a legitimate romance. For example, Mary Kay Letourneau, a married, elementary-school teacher and mother of four children, was sentenced to a 7½-year prison term for sexually abusing a student when he was 12 and she was 34.[3]

- Females who take on babysitting or nanny positions and who then sexually abuse the children in their care. In a study of female adolescent sex offenders, aged 10–18 years, approximately 70 percent of their sexual offenses took place while they were babysitting.[4] In her book, *I'll Scream Later*, Oscar-winning actress Marlee Matlin describes being sexually abused by a 16-year-old female babysitter when she was barely 11.[5]

- Women who abuse children under the age of six, primarily their own. Mother–son incest often consists of subtle forms of sexual activity, such as excessively washing a boy's genitals to the point of stimulation, or massaging a boy's penis to erection.

  In the very rare cases of mother–daughter incest, the mothers have often been severely traumatized themselves during their childhoods, either physically and/or sexually.[6]

Myth #3: Most abusers are homosexuals.

Fact: Heterosexual men commit the majority of childhood sexual abuse. Many abusers are married, often with children of their own, a fact that keeps them "hidden" in plain sight. In reality, when a person molests a child, it has nothing to do with his or her sexual orientation. Homosexual adults are no more likely than heterosexuals to abuse children. Sexual abusers molest children or teenagers because they are sexually attracted to them or use them to meet some other emotional need.

Myth #4: Sexual abusers are usually "dirty old men."

Fact: It's fairly rare for a person to begin sexually abusing children as an older adult. Instead, sexual offending often starts during the adolescent years. It's believed that adolescents are responsible for approximately 40 percent of all sex offenses against children, with most of those adolescents being boys around 14 years of age.[7] Looking back at our portraits in chapter 1, we see that Chris began sexually abusing his sister Laura when he was 14. Juveniles abuse children in their own homes (often their own siblings) or in the child's home (for example, while the teen is babysitting or visiting friends). Adult offenders are not "dirty old men"; they are ordinary people—members of our families, our communities, and our children's lives.

Myth #5: Most abusers are unemployed street people.

Fact: Abusers are rarely unemployed or homeless. People who sexually abuse children come from all walks of life. They are babysitters, bus drivers, coaches, day-care providers, politicians, religious leaders, Scout leaders, teachers, therapists—basically hardworking, ordinary citizens. Daily news headlines illustrate the variety of abusers' occupational backgrounds:

> "Former MLB [major league baseball] player gets 45 years for rape of a minor"[8]
>
> "Stuyvesant Librarian Is Accused of Sexual Abuse: A Stuyvesant High School librarian has been arrested and charged with harassment and sexual abuse after he was accused of inappropriately touching four male students, city investigators said Thursday"[9]
>
> "Frank Lomard, Duke University official, charged in child sex case"[10]
>
> "Man accused of raping daughter held in Hong Kong... former sheriff's deputy"[11]
>
> "Aspen cop, accused of sex crimes and child abuse, resigns"[12]
>
> "Church worker accused of raping girl under 13"[13]
>
> "Child psychiatrist charged with molesting patients"[14]
>
> "Sex predator-teacher pleads guilty to sex with a student"[15]

"Idaho babysitter accused of having sex with 14-year-old"[16]

"Diocese of Scranton priest faces child pornography charges"[17]

Bottom line: Any type of person is capable of sexually abusing a child. Sexual abusers of children come from all racial, ethnic, class, educational, occupational, and religious groups.

Myth #6: Most abusers are mentally ill.

Fact: Anyone who wants to use children for sexual gratification would have to be crazy, psychotic, or mentally ill, right? Contrary to popular belief, not all child sex abusers have the disorder known as pedophilia. A pedophile is a type of abuser who has, usually since adolescence, been sexually attracted to children—an attraction that continues throughout his life. Pedophiles have a sexual preference for children; they think and fantasize about children in sexual ways, have sexual feelings and desires for children, and act on their feelings, desires, and fantasies by using children to obtain sexual gratification. In his book, *Pedophilia and Sexual Offending Against Children*, author Michael Seto estimates that only half of sex offenders who target children are pedophiles.[18] Abusers who are not pedophiles (sometimes called "situational abusers") usually have sexual relations with adults, but in specific situations, they experience a shift in their preference toward a child as a sexual partner. When this shift occurs, they use children sexually to reduce their negative feelings—anxiety, guilt, depression, loneliness, anger, stress, sexual tension, or self-doubt—or to meet their needs for power and control. Mike (from chapter 1) is an example of a situational abuser; he used his stepdaughter Sasha to reduce his negative feelings of resentment, anger, and loneliness.

Myth # 7: Most abusers use physical force to get a child to comply with sexual requests.

Fact: In reality, most cases of childhood sexual abuse do not involve physical force. Instead of force, abusers are more likely to use emotional coercion (for example, threats of harm to child or family, or withdrawal of affection), bribes, or psychological manipulation through offers of friendship, attention, and love. Miss Jenkins, from Monique's story in chapter 1, manipulated Mo by offering to be Mo's friend during a time of need and then showering her with attention.

Myth #8: All abusers were sexually victimized as children.

Fact: Although a large number of offenders say that they were sexually abused as children (73 percent, in one recent study[19]), the other quarter of offenders do not report histories of sexual abuse. Also, most child sexual abuse victims do not grow up and sexually abuse others. It is true, however, that past sexual victimization is a risk factor for later sexual offending, especially if the abuse is not recognized or if the child does not receive help. Mike, from Sasha's story in chapter 1, is an example of how unrecognized childhood sexual abuse, when combined with some stressor in adulthood, can trigger sexual feelings and behaviors toward children. When Mike was a young boy, his female babysitter sexually abused him. Mike did not label what she did to him as abuse, but instead found the experience to be pleasurable and exciting. He was left with the impression that sex between an adult and a child was not really harmful or wrong and certainly not illegal, since there were no legal consequences for what the sitter had done to him. Feelings of physical pleasure coupled with no negative reaction from Sasha led Mike to believe that Sasha would experience the sexual touching as he had as a child, as merely pleasurable and comforting.

Myth #9: Respectable people who do good things would never sexually abuse children.

Fact: Of course abusers appear "nice." Otherwise children would not be drawn to them, nor would parents allow them to be with their children. People who sexually abuse children often lead "double lives"; their private lives and public lives are very different. In terms of their public persona, they are often seen as nice, good, even charming people, as in the following case:

> *When police arrested a 35-year-old music teacher for allegedly fondling a seven-year-old boy while giving him piano lessons in his home, members of the small Florida community rallied around the teacher. Officials at the Arts Academy where the man was employed released a statement regarding the incident. "We are shocked about these allegations. We are a responsible organization that conducts thorough background checks and requires fingerprints prior to employment." Parents also responded with shock to the allegations. A family friend who knew the teacher's wife and three young children told the reporter that the claims are false. "It's a total falsification and it's a horrible thing," said the woman.*[20]

Another case involved U.S. Senator Mark Foley of Florida. At the same time that he was writing legislation to prevent online sexual solicitation of children, he was allegedly using the Internet to prey on teenage boys who had formerly served as Congressional pages. Foley's e-mails to the pages contained sexually explicit conversations. "He didn't want to talk about politics," one page said. "He wanted to talk about sex or my penis."[21] Never prosecuted, Foley resigned from the Senate in September of 2006.

When respected people with impeccable credentials in honorable positions sexually abuse children, the public often reacts with shock and disbelief. People are shocked because they have made assumptions about these people based on their public behavior. They are blindsided by their belief that if a person acts respectful or nice, he or she must be a respectful and nice person, incapable of harming a child. As safety expert and best-selling author Gavin de Becker reminds us, "Niceness is a decision…it is not a character trait."[22] As well as you think you know someone, you can only know what he or she allows you to see.

Bottom Line: You cannot predict private behavior from public behavior.

WHO IS THE TYPICAL CHILD MOLESTER?

So, who is a typical child molester? Here's how child sexual abusers in treatment at the Center for Behavioral Intervention answered that question:

- I am probably well known and liked by you and your child.
- I can be a man or a woman, married or single.
- I can be a child, adolescent, or adult.
- I can be of any race, hold any religious belief, and have any sexual preference.
- I can be a parent, stepparent, relative, family friend, teacher, clergyman, babysitter or anyone who comes in contact with children.
- I am likely to be a stable, employed, respected member of the community.

- My education and my intelligence don't prevent me from molesting your child.
- I can be anybody.[23]

In all likelihood, you already know the person who poses the greatest risk of sexually abusing your child. Nine out of ten times, an abuser is someone a child knows and trusts, and maybe even loves. Abusers cannot be identified based on any outward signs or physical characteristics. They can only be identified by their actions—behaviors that reflect their sexual interest in children. In the next chapter, you will learn how to recognize those behaviors.

Chapter 3

HOW DOES SEXUAL ABUSE HAPPEN?

THE ROLE OF PRIVACY AND AUTHORITY

Engaging a child in sexual activities requires privacy. In most cases of childhood sexual abuse, the abuser is alone with the child. (There are some rare exceptions, such as when a male abuser has a female accomplice, or when one abuser molests multiple children.) Some abusers take advantage of young boys who go by themselves into public restrooms, as this man described: "A great place to hang out is by a toilet in a kiddies' hamburger-type restaurant. Little boys, especially, go into the toilets alone and they aren't expecting someone to try to touch them."[1] Other abusers target children who go places (for example, movies, parks, malls, or video arcades) by themselves.[2] As one abuser who targeted isolated children said, "Children who do not involve themselves with other children during activities or play or who stay to themselves are easy targets. As perpetrators, we spot them and take advantage of the fact that they are not connected to anyone."[3] Another sexual abuser explained that "I never approach children in groups; there are plenty of children on their own. It just isn't worth the risk when there are several kids together, because you can't control them all."[4] Abusers view children who are alone, or who appear not connected to others, as vulnerable children. The next four safety tips propose ways to keep kids and teens off limits to this type of abuser.

OFF LIMITS SAFETY TIP #2:

Teach children and teens a "safety-in-numbers" rule.

Encourage children to travel with a friend—a "safety buddy"—when it's impossible or impractical for an adult to be present. Even when children travel together, remind them never to get into someone's car or go to a home that they do not know. Although implementing the buddy system may be more difficult to do with teenagers, still encourage teens to travel with friends, especially when going to public places.

OFF LIMITS SAFETY TIP #3:

Teach young children what to do if they ever become separated from a parent or person in charge.

Explain to children that if they ever get separated from a caregiver in a store they should:

- stay in the store;
- go to the nearest checkout stand and ask a cashier for help; and
- never leave the premises with someone they do not know.

Be sure children know their first and last names and their parents' first and last names. Also, avoid having children wear clothing or carry items in public that display their names. A person who calls a child by his or her name no longer seems like a stranger to a child.

You can practice this safety skill when you're shopping or visiting a public place with your child. For example, when you're in a store, ask your child to identify someone he could ask for help if he ever got separated from you. Also, ask your child what he would say to that person. Your child will get to practice this skill in a calm situation before he might ever need to ask for help in the much more stressful situation of being separated.

OFF LIMITS SAFETY TIP #4:

Avoid letting young children go alone into public restrooms.

Have an adult accompany a young child (approximately age seven or under) into a public restroom. With an opposite-sex child, taking him with you into your gender's bathroom becomes more difficult as he gets older. If no adults or safety buddies are available to accompany your older child, let him go alone into a public restroom, and wait close by for his safe return. It is good for parents to speak to their children from outside the bathroom door so the child appears connected to an adult.

OFF LIMITS SAFETY TIP #5:

Teach children to always "ask first."

Teach children to ask first (get permission from a parent or another trusted adult) before agreeing to do something, going somewhere, accepting anything (like gifts or money), getting into a vehicle, or helping anyone who's not a family member (for example, responding to requests for directions, time, help finding a lost pet, etc.). In her exceptionally informative book, *Identifying Child Molesters*, author Carla van Dam describes how Mr. Clay, a teacher, would ask children to help him out after school.[5] Those children who wanted to call their parents and ask for permission to stay after school were not abused, but the children who didn't ask for parental permission were. By implementing this safety tip, these parents eliminated their children as targets. An "ask first" rule applies to older children and teenagers, as well. When older children and teens leave home, request that they tell you where they are going, who they will be with, and when they will return. Also ask them to let you know if they make any changes to their plans.

POWER AND AUTHORITY

All of the abusers we portrayed in chapter 1 had power and authority over the children they abused. They were all in positions of authority and trust (as a teacher, stepfather, babysitter, or youth pastor), and they took advantage of that authority to control Mo, Sasha, Laura, and Gustavo. Along with privacy, power and authority are the most important ingredients that enable a person to coerce a child into sexual compliance. Some abusers purposefully place themselves in settings and activities that offer easy access to and privacy with children. If they are also in positions of authority, then they can misuse their authority to control children. Homes, schools, churches, and youth organizations (for example, Scouts, sporting leagues) offer plenty of opportunities for abusers to be alone with children, and they are the most common places children are sexually abused. Although these are the most common places, children can be sexually abused anywhere. Children have been abused in cars, movie theaters, hospitals, public restrooms, airplanes, ambulances, swimming pools, and many other places. The next three safety tips address the main risk factors of privacy and misuse of authority.

OFF LIMITS SAFETY TIP #6:

Make careful choices about allowing children to be alone with an authority figure.

Question the motives and intentions of any authority figure who seems overly interested in kids and who spends a lot of spare time alone with them. Most adults' friends are other adults, not children. Even when adults spend their working hours with kids, they don't usually spend their personal time alone with them. Teachers or other school personnel have no reason to socialize alone with children on weekends, after school, or in the evenings. Nor is there any reason for adult leaders of youth organizations or coaches to be spending time alone with children outside of their normal job responsibilities. A child may be thrilled to be invited by his leader or coach to go to his home, out for pizza, or to a movie, but it is inappropriate and potentially unsafe.

Here's how one sexual abuser—a sixth-grade teacher—used his professional authority to obtain access to children. According to this teacher, "Parents literally give us their children. Permission slips for field trips, camping stay-overs, after-school tutoring, and so on, are automatically signed without ever having met me or knowing anything about me. A parent gives permission simply because I'm his teacher. I've even called their homes and asked to keep their son overnight for tutoring, and they always agreed. They sure made it easy for me."[6]

Don't make it easy for an abuser. Do not allow a child to go somewhere alone with an authority figure. Don't allow the child to spend the night with the adult, travel places alone with him, take vacations with him, visit his home, or socialize with him outside of official group activities. If an authority figure proposes a one-on-one activity with a child, learn all that is possible about that person and try to determine the individual's particular interest in the child. If possible, request that additional supervisors be present. Then, when the child returns from the activity, be sure to discuss all the details of the excursion, not in an interrogating fashion, but by expressing sincere interest in the activity.

What about situations where it's within the person's job description to be alone with a child? Music teachers, for example, have access to children in private environments. Here's an example of how a music teacher took advantage of the privacy he was granted:

> *Investigative reporter Jace Larson from KUSA 9NEWS in Denver, Colorado, describes how Mark, a former music teacher, was able to molest over 200 children during a 25-year period. Mark offered music lessons in his home so that he could be alone with children, one-on-one. "I could [use the lessons for] physical touching, often disguised as 'open your mouth wider' or 'use your stomach more.' I would touch them in places that might have otherwise been questionable to them," said Mark. "The more I did that, the easier it was to do more." Mark told 9NEWS, "The thing that still amazes me [is that] I never ever recall a single occasion where a parent of a boy I was targeting this way ever came to my house, ever came to see where it was that I was taking him. If they had, it would have terrified me to death. Even if they would have just brought him over and said, 'Hey, can I see your house?' it would have been very disturbing and frightening to me that they were suspicious, and I probably would have stopped."*[7]

When you first bring tutors into your home, try to stay within earshot and eyesight. If your child goes to the teacher's home or office for lessons, stay there and supervise, or, if you cannot go, have some other adult there in your place.

As Mark in the example above recommends, drop in unannounced to see how the lessons are going.

Although we recommend avoiding situations where children are alone with authority figures, the reality is that children will be alone with those authority figures a great many times (including with their own parents as well as siblings, relatives, teachers, or family friends). To further reduce the power of an "unsafe" authority figure, consider implementing the following safety tip.

OFF LIMITS SAFETY TIP #7:

Make sure your children know that they do not have to comply with unsafe or inappropriate requests from an authority figure.

Children who are taught blind obedience to adult authority are more vulnerable to abuse. Sherry was one such child. Her parents had taught her to always respect and obey adults, but a "trusted" neighbor took advantage of her blind obedience and sexually abused her. Sherry reflected back on that experience in a thought-provoking article in *Redbook* magazine: "I was compelled by the misconception that I had to obey [the neighbor] because he was an adult. I had been taught to respect my elders, and feared that if I challenged his authority, I would be the one who was punished—either by him or by my parents."[8] Many parents automatically remind children to "be good" and "follow rules" when they leave their children with authority figures, as in the following example:

> *A father drops his son off at school and says, "Be a good boy today. Mind the teacher. Follow all the rules and do everything your teacher tells you to do." But if a teacher who was a sex offender heard the father say, "Mind the teacher," the teacher might then say to the child, "Let's go in the computer room and play a fun touching game." In this situation, a parent's instruction to obey put this child at risk for sexual abuse.*

Children need permission to say "No" to any authority figure who asks them to do something that's not safe, that could endanger them, or that would break a body-safety rule (described in chapter 6).

Implementing this safety tip with your children may be challenging if your cultural or religious background stresses the importance of children respecting and obeying their elders. Your task is to teach your children that although respecting elders is important, they can still say "No" to anyone (including elders or relatives) whom they think might jeopardize their safety. The message to a child should always be that safety comes first, and manners second.

Such a GOOD little girl I was. I learned to respect authority: Trust adults. Don't talk back. Don't ask questions. Listen to your elders. Be quiet. Mind your manners. Be a lady. Don't make a scene. Do what you're told. So I was molested at five by a relative, molested at seven by a neighbor, raped at 19 by a co-worker. Good Little Girls Make Great Little Victims—TEACH YOUR CHILDREN TO SPEAK UP![9]

—Joni (age 30), San Diego, 1993

EXPLOITING AUTHORITY INSIDE THE HOME

The majority of childhood sexual abuse cases occur in homes—most often in the child's own home, but also in the abuser's home.[10] Children are sexually abused by people who live in or visit their homes—parents, stepparents, grandparents, foster parents, mothers' boyfriends, siblings, other relatives, parents' friends, sitters and nannies, and in-home tutors. In the case of incest, the abuser is already in a position of trust and has immediate access to potential victims. All of these people occupy positions of authority and find it simple to obtain privacy with a child.

Once Mike lost his job and became Sasha's primary caretaker, he was alone with her often—after school, in the evenings, and on weekends. He had all the privacy he needed to molest her. So did Chris, Laura's older brother. While their parents were at work, Chris took advantage of the privacy and authority he was afforded through his babysitting responsibilities.

People have many opportunities to be alone with children and to sexually abuse them in their own homes. Just like you safety-proof your home by installing stair gates, outlet covers, or locking the pool gate, you can abuse-proof your home by implementing the following safety tip, which is one of many ways you can create an off limits home.

OFF LIMITS SAFETY TIP #8:

Grant all family members the right to privacy.

In Laura and Chris's home, rights to privacy were not enforced. Without their permission and against their wishes, Chris would frequently barge into his sisters' bedrooms while they were undressing. Then he started going into the bathroom while Laura was showering, saying he needed to use the toilet. When family members do not respect each other's privacy, physical boundaries can be crossed, and the risk for sexual abuse increases. All family members should be entitled to privacy when they are bathing, dressing, sleeping, using the toilet, and doing other personal activities. Sometimes parents' beliefs about children's rights to privacy can unintentionally teach the wrong messages and can possibly put their children at risk for sexual abuse. Following is a conversation between a four-year-old boy and his mother, in a women's locker room, for you to consider:

Child: "Mommy, I have to pee."
Mother (opening the bathroom door): "Okay, sweetie, go pee."
Child: "Mommy, will you shut the door?"
Mother: "Just go pee."
Child: "But Mom, please, shut the door."
Mother (frustrated, emphatically says): "Just go pee."
Child uses toilet and comes out of the stall.
Mother: "Sweetie, I need to use the toilet, so come in with me and shut the door."
Child: "But Mom, you didn't let me shut the door."
Mother: "I said come in here. Adults need privacy; children don't. Now get in here and shut the door."

Nothing could be further from the truth. Children need privacy as much as adults do.

How can parents grant children the right to privacy? You might show them by example how to ask for privacy. If you're in the bathroom with the door closed, and your child walks in without knocking, you can say, "Please knock before coming into the bathroom when I'm using it. I'd like my privacy now, so please go out and close the door. I'll be out in a few minutes." Later, explain the concept of privacy (that it is when you want to be alone, and not have company).

Teach your child that a closed door means, "Knock before entering." Many children at a certain age (usually around five) go through a modesty stage where they start requesting privacy, particularly during toileting and dressing. You can take advantage of this natural modesty by granting your children's requests for privacy (as long as it does not compromise their safety). For example, if your five-year-old wants to use the toilet with the door closed, allow her to do so as long as you are close by in case she needs help. And make sure to respect your child's privacy. If the bathroom door is shut, knock first, and wait to be invited in. If you respect your children's rights to privacy, then they will learn to expect the same from others.

OFF LIMITS SAFETY TIP #9:

Allow children to choose how they demonstrate affection.

Some parents expect their children to give and receive physical affection when told to do so, especially with relatives. Following is a common scenario when Grandma, who lives across the country, has just arrived to visit her grandson:

> *Dad says to his child, "Grandma's here. Go give her a kiss!"*
> *Child says, "I don't want to."*
> *Dad responds, "Go give her a kiss, now!"*
> *Child whines, "But I don't want to!"*
> *Dad insists, "You'll hurt her feelings if you don't give her a k*iss!"

Dad's final statement sends a powerful message to his son—basically, that Grandma's feelings are more important than his son's feelings, and that the child must please Grandma. Sometimes children are simply not in the mood to show affection to loved ones, not because the loved one is an abuser, but perhaps because Grandma's perfume smells funny, or Grandpa's face is scratchy, or the child just doesn't feel like it. It's important to respect a child's choice about sharing his body, even with a grandma he may see only once a year. A child who is not permitted to resist physical affection in a safe situation—kissing a doting grandparent—may have difficulty resisting physical affection in an unsafe situation. That's because of the underlying messages being conveyed (that a child must please an adult, never hurt an adult's feelings, and always do what an adult wants, regardless of the request). For instance, what if a favorite uncle who intends to sexually abuse his niece says, "If you really love me, you'll sit on my lap and kiss me." A child who has been taught that she must hug and kiss loved ones is vulnerable to this type of ploy. On the other hand, children who are permitted to express affection on their own terms and to assertively refuse unwanted affection will be better able to resist a touch or kiss that they do not want.

One parent shared her struggle implementing this safety tip when she said, "In my culture, we are very huggy and touchy when our family gets together. We all kiss and hug each other. How do I now tell my child she can choose whom she hugs and kisses when it's just what we do?" From the perspective of sexual abuse prevention, it is important to teach children in all cultures that they have the right to choose how they show affection to others. We aren't suggesting that you tell your children not to kiss or hug their relatives. What we are suggesting is that you explain to your children that if they do not want to kiss or hug a relative, it's okay, and that they have many other ways to show affection and to communicate love and respect. Children can be respectful of and affectionate with loved ones without kissing and hugging. For example, they can acknowledge loved ones by saying, "Hi," waving, blowing a kiss, bowing, or shaking hands. Children vary in their comfort levels regarding physical touch—some kids are very cuddly and affectionate, others are not—so it's important for children to decide for themselves how they want to express affection with loved ones. In the previous scenario of Grandma visiting, Dad might have asked his son (before she arrived), "How would you like to greet Grandma?" Of course you need to prepare Grandma for this. You might explain to Grandma why you are giving your child a choice about showing affection. Invite Grandma to join your family's prevention team, so she feels empowered, rather than hurt.

Sometimes we give children mixed messages about their right to give and receive affection. How many times have you said to a child, "Give me a kiss goodnight," or "Where's my hug?" or "Go kiss your dad/grandma goodnight"? We expect the child to do as we ask and show affection to us or to others. To truly grant children the right to choose how they show affection, try asking kids for permission to get or receive physical affection. Instead of saying, "Give me a kiss goodnight," you might say, "May I have a kiss goodnight?" Every time you ask "May I?" or "Can I?" you are giving children a choice. Of course we have to respect their choice, even if it means that we don't get our hug or kiss. It may be difficult to respect a child's response of "No," but giving children the choice of giving or receiving physical affection teaches them how to be assertive and potentially be seen as off limits to abusers.

Bottom line: Just as adults get to choose whom they hug and kiss, so should children be able to.

Consider this scenario:

> *You and your spouse are in the grocery store standing in the check-out line. Along comes your good friend Raya. Your spouse hasn't seen your friend in months, and you say, "Oh sweetie, there's Raya. Go give her a kiss!"*

Can you imagine saying that to your adult partner? Yet adults often make requests like this of their children. And when they do, children experience a double standard. Adults can choose when, how, and if to give or receive physical affection, but sometimes we don't give children that choice. Through learning that they have choices about how and when they display affection, your children will come to understand that they truly have the right to keep their bodies off limits. Much like a teenager posts a NO TRESPASSING sign on his or her bedroom door, you can help a child post an imaginary sign on his or her body that says NO TRESPASSING ALLOWED!

Chapter 4

GAINING SEXUAL COMPLIANCE

Once an abuser has the important ingredients of privacy, authority, control, and trust in place with a child, then the abuser attempts to gain sexual compliance. Abusers employ a variety of strategies to get children to comply with their sexual requests. First they develop a friendship and give children lots of love and attention. They become "best friends"—talking and listening and encouraging the child to share any worries or concerns. As one sexual abuser told his interviewer, "By listening to a boy, sharing secrets, and encouraging him to talk about everything that was on his mind, he usually wanted to spend time with me, and inadvertently provided me with all that I needed to know about his vulnerabilities to victimize him."[1]

Monique experienced firsthand these skilled manipulations by her volleyball coach and teacher, as we read in chapter 1. In the early stage of their relationship, Mo described Miss Jenkins as her confidante. Mo felt comfortable talking to Miss Jenkins about her feelings, and Miss Jenkins really seemed interested in what Mo had to say. Miss Jenkins also bought her things like tennis shoes and even paid for Mo's uniform when her parents couldn't afford to. Miss Jenkins would always say that these were just her way of showing Mo how much she loved her. Just as Miss Jenkins had done with Mo, some abusers give children and teenagers gifts—stuffed animals, bikes, movie tickets, clothes, music, money, cell phones, computer games, admission to family fun centers or amusement parks—with the hope of getting something in return. Indeed, most of the child victims who were interviewed by researchers Lucy Berliner and Jon Conte described being given special favors, money, or clothes by their abusers.[2] The time, attention, and gifts are ways to emotionally seduce the child so that the child feels indebted to the person.

OFF LIMITS SAFETY TIP #10:

Take notice when someone shows lots of attention to one particular child or showers that child with gifts.

Be aware of a person (not related to your child) who gives her lots of gifts. It would be fine for a schoolteacher to give each student in his class a notebook, but it is not appropriate for a teacher to lavish one particular student with gifts. Take note if a child has acquired new toys, money, computer games, or clothes. Ask where these items came from, and carefully listen to her response. Also, tune in to your child's comments about the people she spends time with (those who are in a position of authority). Pay attention if your child talks a lot about her "special friend."

OFF LIMITS SAFETY TIP #11:

Actively listen to children.

Active listening means carefully paying attention to what a child is saying, both verbally and nonverbally. It means "listening" with your ears and eyes. "Listening" with your eyes means watching a child's nonverbal behavior—posture, facial expressions (smiles, frowns), and eye contact—because these behaviors communicate a lot. Active listening also involves asking children questions, or asking them to expand or clarify what they are saying, or asking them to explain things to you in a different way.

Here's an example of a parent not actively listening to his child:

> *Jack and his five-year-old daughter, Tammy, are driving in the car. Tammy says, "Dad, when is Julie coming back?" [Julie is the babysitter.]*
> *Jack replies, "Oh, Julie is coming back next week."*
> *Tammy responds, "I don't want Julie to come back."*
> *Her dad reassures her, "You love Julie and Julie loves you. You have so much fun with her."*
> *Tammy responds, "No, I don't like her."*
> *Her dad replies, "That's not nice. You do like her and you shouldn't say mean things about Julie."*

Jack missed an important opportunity to actively listen and find out what Tammy's worries, concerns, or fears were about her sitter.

Let's look at how an "active-listening" Jack might have responded to her question:

> *"Dad, when is Julie coming back?"*
> *"I don't know sweetie, why do you ask?"*
> *"I don't want Julie to come back."*
> *"Why don't you want Julie to come back?"*
> *"Because she's mean to me."*
> *"How is she mean to you?"*
> *"Well, when Julie watches me, her boyfriend comes over and they touch my private parts and I don't like it."*
> *"Tammy, I'm very proud of you for telling me. I will make sure that never happens again."*

As you can see, asking lots of "how" and "why" questions can make it possible for a parent to understand a child's real concerns and to intervene to prevent any further abuse.

In the beginning of his relationship with his youth pastor, Gustavo tried to tell his mother that Kevin was touching him by saying, "Kevin's gay." What's not clear from this comment is whether he was making fun of Kevin or if he was telling his mom that he was being abused. It's important for a parent to find out what a child means by these kinds of vague statements. Gustavo's mother could have asked, "How do you know that?" or "What do you mean by that?" A child who was being abused might have responded, "'Cuz he touches me." Hearing your child say that he has been sexually touched by a trusted adult would be difficult for any parent, yet the real tragedy would be if a child tried to disclose the information but was not heard. In response to Gustavo's comment, his mom scolded him for talking about Kevin "that way" and reminded him how much everybody loved and respected Kevin. Unfortunately, her response closed the door to any further disclosure, and the abuse continued.

SEXUALIZING THE RELATIONSHIP

Once the abuser establishes an emotional bond with the child, then the relationship becomes sexual. One common tactic is to add sexual contact to an already established routine of nonsexual touching. Physical contacts often begin in nonsexual ways (through tickling, cuddling, wrestling, roughhousing, hugging, back rubs, or massages). Mike's relationship with Sasha included a lot of physical contact that was nonsexual at first (lots of cuddling and tickling as a way of showing fatherly affection), but over time, that behavior led to sexually stimulating contact and eventually to intercourse. In his book, *Unspeakable Acts*, Douglas Pryor describes how a man named Leon first began molesting his stepdaughter when she was around eight.[3] The sexual contact occurred while the two sat together in a recliner chair and watched television in the evenings. Leon began with affectionate holding and caressing (rubbing her legs and stomach) and then slowly progressed to touching and then fondling her genitals. Like Leon, Mike's touches of Sasha also slowly progressed from nonsexual to sexual. While bathing her, he spent more time washing her genitals than he did the rest of her body. As she got older, they began taking showers together, where it was easy for him to convince her to "help wash Daddy."

Another early strategy is to "accidentally" touch a child's genitals, perhaps while giving a massage or drying a child off after a bath. The person might touch the child's genitals but then apologize, saying it was an accident. One child victim described this technique by saying, "He accidentally on purpose comes in the bedroom or bathroom when you're undressed, or accidentally on purpose touches your private parts, or accidentally on purpose shows you his body naked."[4] Mike used "accidental touches" to blur the boundaries between nurturing and sexual touches with Sasha. As Sasha's body developed, Mike started "accidentally" touching her genitals during back rubs and massages. Such seemingly "innocent" touches may look harmless, but they have a specific purpose—to desensitize the child to physical contact and to blur the boundaries between appropriate and inappropriate touches.

OFF LIMITS SAFETY TIP #12:

Know the difference between healthy displays of affection and sexual types of touching.

Obviously, not every person who hugs, tickles, wrestles, or roughhouses with kids is intending to abuse them. In fact, young children in general and boys in particular usually like to play physically with adults, and most of the time, such contact play is safe, healthy, and fun. A sexual abuser's play with children, however, has some unique characteristics. First, the play usually involves more than the average amount of physical contact, almost as if the person is obsessed with touching children. Second, the child rarely initiates or suggests the touching games; it's usually the abuser who "choreographs" the play activities. Third, and most concerning, the person fails to respect a child's request to stop.

These early visible touching behaviors are the first indicators that the person may be leading up to sexually abusive behaviors. One child abuser considered tickling and roughhousing to be such a significant indicator of crossing boundaries that he recommended adults have a zero-tolerance policy regarding such contact with children.[5] Should you see someone excessively tickling and roughhousing with a child, especially if these behaviors coexist with other warning signs like a person trying to arrange time alone with a child, or a person seeming to be obsessed with touching children, then take action. If these types of touches are misunderstood and no one intervenes, it gives abusers a green light to escalate the type and extent of physical contact.

You may experience situations in which you're not 100 percent sure that a child is being set up for abuse, but ones that nevertheless cause you to feel uneasy or uncomfortable. For example, one parent told us that she was concerned about her child's preschool teacher who was always tickling the children, including her son, even though her son tried, in his biggest three-year-old voice, to tell the teacher that he didn't want to be tickled. This teacher also wouldn't allow parents to visit his classroom unannounced. What could she or any parent do in this situation? Consider the following options:

Talk to other parents. Share your concerns and describe the questionable behaviors you have seen. Ask other parents if they have noticed similar behaviors or if their children have ever complained about this teacher. Trade information with other parents, and document what is discussed. Sharing this type of information is not gossiping; the goal of responsible communication is to keep children safe.

Talk to the teacher's supervisor. Describe what you've seen and ask what other parents have reported. Request that the supervisor talk to the teacher in question. If the teacher's inappropriate behavior continues, consider talking to the director of the facility, or contacting an official in law enforcement or social services and describing your concerns.

Speak to experts who specialize in child sexual abuse issues. The expert could be a therapist, social worker, psychologist, family doctor, or someone at a children's advocacy center or social services department. Such professionals can help you decide what to do, including whether or not to speak to the teacher directly.

Speak to the teacher. If you are comfortable asking about a behavior that may fall in the "gray" area—not obviously sexual abuse, but still questionable—you might consider asking the teacher himself about the behavior. What can you say? First, make sure you don't accuse the teacher of anything specific or use labels such as "sex abuser" or "child molester." These labels will put the teacher on the defensive. Instead, focus on the behaviors you have seen or the language you have heard. For example, the parent who noticed the preschool teacher excessively tickling her son might say to him, "My son really loves playing with you, but I am uncomfortable when you tickle him and won't stop when he asks you to. Is there a reason you don't stop tickling him when he asks you to stop?" You can learn a great deal about a person by his response to this type of questioning. A person who genuinely cares about a child would be concerned about how the behavior affected the child. If the teacher replies, "Wow, I had no idea my tickling upset him. I'll apologize to him right away, and never do that again," that's a very different response than if he says, "Your son needs to get tougher. He's too much of a crybaby." Or if he says, "You know, kids lie about that stuff all the time." These kinds of defensive reactions should be viewed as red flags. If the teacher tries to convince you that the tickling is a harmless game, inform his supervisor about this interaction. Be sure to tell the teacher that you do not want him tickling your child. You could do so by saying, "My son really loves playing with you, but I do not want you tickling him anymore."

Like touches, conversations also can become sexualized. During interviews, several children described how their abusers used "sex" talk.[6] They would say things like "He'd tell me I had beautiful legs," "He'd tell me I looked sexy in my shorts," or "He said I had a nice body and ought to show it off." Sexual abusers report that they would carefully test the child's reaction to sex by bringing up sexual matters, telling off-color jokes, showing or taking pornographic pictures or movies, talking about their own sexual experiences, or "teaching" the child about sex. Another child told interviewers, "He was teaching me how to do all the stuff so that when I got older and got married and stuff, I would know how to keep my body satisfied."[7] Kevin also talked about sex with Gustavo, once he began showing signs of entering puberty. As a "father figure," Kevin began talking to Gustavo about sex, asking him if he ever woke up with an erection or ever had a wet dream. Chris made Laura look at porn sites on the Internet and then told her to do the same things to him that she had seen on the sites. And a 36-year-old incestuous father told author Linda Sanford that "I just wanted to teach her [his daughter] about sex. I wanted her to learn from someone who knew what he was doing and wouldn't get her pregnant. I didn't want her first experience to be with some careless, irresponsible teenage boy."[8]

By now, the abuser has usually gained the child's trust, established opportunities to be alone with the child, and crossed the boundary of appropriate touch and conversation into inappropriate sexual talk and sexual activities. The touch may have moved from on top of the child's clothes to underneath and from hugs to caresses of the genitals. Now the abuser must ensure that the activities can continue without being discovered, which, in the abuser's mind, depends on a child's willingness to keep secrets. In the next chapter, we describe how abusers sustain the secrecy.

CHAPTER 5

KEEPING THE SECRET

Sexual abuse of a child requires secrecy. Some abusers "train" children to keep secrets by first asking the child to keep innocent secrets. Here's how Alan, a pedophile interviewed by author Amy Hammel-Zabin, used secrets. "My methods were designed to build, very slowly, a child's acceptance of the need for secrets. At the same time, secrecy gave me the opportunity to make a child believe that I was the only person in the world who really cared for him and looked out for him. I would test the boy to see if he had the ability to keep a secret. I would, for example, swear in front of him. Having done this, I would explain that I should not have and would ask him to keep my mistake just between the two of us. I waited to see if he did, in fact, keep quiet about the incident. If he didn't, I would then immediately end all attempts at victimizing him. On the other hand, if after a week it was clear that this secret had been kept, I escalated the process. Keeping all of these seemingly minor secrets built up a feeling of equal responsibility and equal guilt in this totally innocent child."[1]

Like Alan, Kevin used secrecy to entice Gustavo. Seeing how often the other boys in the church class teased him, Kevin began testing Gustavo's willingness to keep innocent secrets by confiding in him about some of the other boys' troubles. He would share private information about the boys and their families, telling Gustavo not to disclose the information to anyone else. One boy was having problems in school, Kevin told Gus, while another boy's parents were getting divorced, and the biggest bully of all was still wetting his bed at night. Kevin said that the reason he was telling Gustavo these things was because he needed to talk to someone about the responsibilities he was carrying, because the stresses in his job were too much to bear alone. Gustavo felt very special to be trusted with this information. As they spent more time together, Kevin began to ask Gustavo to keep more secrets. When they went to R-rated movies containing sexual language and nudity, Kevin instructed Gustavo not to tell the church leaders because they wouldn't approve. When Gustavo spent weekends at Kevin's house, Kevin would let Gustavo drink alcohol and smoke pot with him, but he made him promise never to tell anyone, saying he'd get fired if anyone found out. Over time, Gustavo became trapped by Kevin's secrets and felt that if he told, then both of them would be in a great deal of trouble.

OFF LIMITS SAFETY TIP #13:

Establish a "no-secrets" rule in your home.

To keep your children safe from sexual abuse, consider establishing a "no-secrets" rule in your home. Enforcing this rule can be challenging. One reason why it's difficult to implement this rule is that family members often ask children to keep seemingly "harmless" secrets: for example, when Grandma says, "Don't tell your dad I let you have an ice cream cone before dinner," or when Dad says, "Don't tell your mom that I got a speeding ticket." Asking children to keep secrets teaches them that it's acceptable to keep secrets. Children may then think it's okay to comply with an abuser's request to keep the touching "our special secret."

To help kids avoid keeping unsafe secrets, you can make a "no-secrets" rule by telling young children never to keep secrets from you. You can say, "We don't keep secrets in our family." That way a child knows that if anyone requests that an activity be kept secret, the child will recognize the secret keeping as something wrong and can say, "We don't keep secrets in my family."

Following is how the "no-secrets" rule worked in Meg's family. Meg's daughter, Nikki (age five), attended an after-school gymnastics class. Here's a conversation that occurred between Nikki and her gymnastics teacher:

Teacher: Let's make up a dance and keep it our special secret. Let's not tell your mom or anyone else about our dance.

Nikki: But we don't keep secrets in my family.

"If your mother asks, we crossed at the corner."

Teacher: What do you mean you don't keep secrets?

Nikki: I'm not allowed to keep secrets from my mom. I tell her everything.

Nikki went home and told her mother about the gymnastics teacher's request. Meg praised her daughter for telling and immediately contacted the teacher to let him know that she was uncomfortable with any adult asking her child to keep secrets. After the teacher minimized and dismissed Meg's concerns, Meg removed her daughter from the class. Meg will never know if his request for keeping the dance a secret was innocent or if the teacher was using the "keeping secrets" tactic to set her daughter up for molestation. If he was a sexual abuser, however, this mother's message was loud and clear: "My child is off limits to you!"

Instead of keeping secrets, parents can teach their children that it's okay to keep surprises. To explain the difference between secrets and surprises, you can say, "Surprises are things that, after a while, you tell someone about, and it makes that person happy. A surprise might be a birthday gift for your friend. You don't tell your friend what the present is—for a little while. Then you give her the gift and she is surprised and happy. But secrets are things people might tell you to keep to yourself and never tell anyone about. In our family, it's okay to keep surprises, but it's not okay to keep secrets." Make the difference obvious. Secrets are never told, but surprises are most fun when they are told!

A very concrete "no-secrets" rule is best with young children under the age of six or seven. With older children you might teach them the difference between safe and unsafe secrets. You could say, "Safe secrets (or surprises), like presents and parties, are fun to keep. Unsafe secrets don't feel good to keep. Those are secrets that someone asks you never to tell. You should always tell an adult if someone asks you to keep an unsafe secret." Preteens and teenagers are better able to understand which kinds of secrets are appropriate and safe to keep, and which ones are not. As a result, you can have more abstract conversations with older children about things like keeping information private or confidential. Here are some examples you can use to help teenagers understand what type of secrets can be kept private:

> **Question:** What if your friend tells you he wants to date a girl in his gym class but asks you not to tell anyone? Is that okay to keep private?
>
> **Answer:** Yes—because the secret does not jeopardize the girl's safety.
>
> **Question:** What if your teacher tells you that if you kiss her, she'll give you an A on your report card? Is that okay to keep private?
>
> **Answer:** No—because a kiss between a teacher and student is inappropriate and legally wrong and needs to be disclosed.
>
> **Question [for girls]:** What if your friend tells you she just started her period and doesn't want anyone else to know? Is that okay to keep private?
>
> **Answer:** Yes—because the secret does not jeopardize her safety.
>
> **Question [for boys]:** What if your buddy tells you he had a wet dream last night but asks you not to tell anyone? Is that okay to keep private?

Answer: Yes—because the secret does not jeopardize his safety.

Question: What if your friend tells you that her dad walks around the house in his boxer shorts, and when he sits down to watch TV, his penis is exposed? Your friend feels uncomfortable about it. Is it okay to keep this private?

Answer: No—because the friend feels uncomfortable.

Question: What if your friend tells you that her stepfather touches her body at night, and your friend makes you promise never to tell anyone? Is that okay to keep private?

Answer: No—because this is inappropriate and legally wrong and needs to be disclosed.

This last example is a common one—teenagers who are being sexually abused often confide in their friends instead of adults. Often, teens will ask friends to keep their disclosures secret, or they make the friends promise not to tell adults, sometimes threatening to end the friendship if the other friend tells. Help your teen understand that this kind of secret should never be kept. Here's how you could describe the need to break confidentiality: "If a friend ever asks you to keep an unsafe secret, it's important that you don't keep it and instead talk to an adult you trust. You'll be more of a hero by helping your friend than by keeping the secret or protecting your friendship." It takes a lot of courage for a teen to jeopardize the friendship by telling an adult. Remember that abusers count on kids keeping secrets, so do your best to let kids know they never have to keep unsafe secrets—their own or others'.

OFF LIMITS SAFETY TIP #14:

Know how abusers keep children from telling.

Once the friendship becomes sexualized, abusers must make sure children do not tell anyone about the abuse. They get this guarantee in a variety of ways. Some use psychological manipulation or mind games, such as convincing the child that he had willingly participated in the sexual activity and would therefore be equally blamed if he told. The priest who molested Barbara Blaine (whom we met in chapter 1) blamed her for tempting him. She carried that shame and guilt with her for decades. Some abusers explicitly tell children not to reveal "our special secret." Others use threats involving physical harm (for example, to harm the other children in the home). Two of the abusers interviewed by Douglas Pryor each said they told their victims not to say anything to their mothers, or else their mothers would "kill" both of them.[2] Others used threats about what would happen to the offender ("You don't want to get me in trouble—I could go to jail"). Incest offenders (especially fathers) often threaten abandonment or rejection ("We'll get divorced, and the family will fall apart" or "You'll have to go to a foster home").

In our opening stories, Mike told his stepdaughter Sasha that her "love" kept him from straying, and in her mind she felt like she was keeping the family together. And Kevin, the youth pastor, used a variety of threats with Gustavo. He made Gustavo believe that going to R-rated movies, drinking alcohol, and smoking pot were Gustavo's choice, making Gustavo as much of a culprit as Kevin. Later on, Kevin used religion to silence Gustavo, telling him that if he told anyone about the drinking and touching, God would be disappointed in him. Gustavo didn't want anyone, especially God, to be disappointed in him, and this threat kept him silent for years.

Here are some of the threats abusers use to keep children from telling. For each one, imagine a child is hearing these words, and feel the power behind the threats.

"If you tell…

- you'll be sorrier than you've ever been in your life."
- you'll be taken away."
- no one will believe you."
- everybody will think it's your fault."
- I'll go to jail and you won't see me anymore."
- I will hurt you [your little sister, your Mom/Dad, your pet]." (Threats to harm family members are especially powerful and effective.)
- Mom will be really mad at both of us, and I'll get kicked out of the house."

- your mom and I are going to end up in a divorce, we'll lose our home, and you'll have to change schools and leave your friends."
- you'll have to go to a foster home."

Sometimes abusers don't need to explicitly threaten or demand that a child keep abuse a secret. Some abusers take advantage of the fact that young children are cognitively unable to understand sexual acts or recognize an abuser's sexual intentions. These children do not tell because they do not know that the sexual activity is wrong. Other children say that the person gave them a "look" that effectively silenced them. Older children may know that what's happening is wrong because of the way they feel (embarrassed or dirty). But it is difficult for victims to tell someone about abuse when they feel dirty, damaged, or ashamed. These feelings are often sufficient to assure silence, especially among adolescents.

Sometimes abusers use bribes (for example, money or special privileges) to reward secret keeping. Another reason children don't tell anyone is that they may love, adore, depend on, or occasionally worship the person who is sexually abusing them. Why would a child who is being sexually abused by her father/teacher/coach want to protect her abuser? Listen to the reasons given by these survivors of childhood sexual abuse. Incest survivor Marilyn Van Derbur writes, "My father was all I had. As destructive and as soul murdering as his attention was at night, it was the only attention I received. To believe that my father never loved me during the day, that he only used me for his own pleasures at night, would be to feel a sense of abandonment so deep, so agonizing, it would have destroyed me completely."[3] In chapter 1, Mo experienced very conflicted feelings toward Miss Jenkins—liking and respecting her, but hating what she was doing to her. And like Mo, Sasha was confused by her stepfather's sexual touching and wanted it to stop, but she did not want to lose Mike's love and affection.

Because of looks, threats, bribes, shame, warnings not to tell, and adoration for the person, most children keep the sexual activity a secret. In fact, only 10 percent of children ever report their abuse while it's happening.[4] Right before Christmas in 2008, a nine-year-old girl in a Texas community revealed her sexual abuse in a letter she wrote to Santa Claus. She asked Santa to make a relative stop touching her and her sister. The girl turned the letter in at her elementary school and the school's counselor reported the letter to the authorities, who arrested a man for molesting the two girls over a four-year period.[5] Most children do not tell about their abuse for years; some never do.

Boys are particularly reluctant to tell anyone about their abuse. Society expects boys to be tough, strong, dominant, and able to defend themselves. They are not supposed to express helplessness or vulnerability. Cross-cultural expert Lisa Aronson Fontes describes how young Latino men may perceive that being sexually abused tarnishes their masculinity and diminishes their social worth.[6] Gustavo felt so ashamed and embarrassed that he did not disclose his abuse by Kevin until he was in his mid-50s. Another explanation for lower reporting rates among boys is the possibility of greater shame and the fear that they will be labeled as homosexual (if the abuser was a male) or weak (if the abuser was a female). Such fears can keep boys quiet, as happened with Gustavo.

When it's a woman who sexually abuses a boy, sometimes people view it as a boy's sexual rite of passage or as "every young boy's fantasy." If you're not sure whether a 14-year-old boy having sex with a 30-year-old female teacher is sexual abuse, then imagine a 14-year-old girl having sex with a 30-year-old male teacher. Is that sexual abuse? Regardless of the victim's gender, whenever an older, more knowledgeable, and more powerful person exploits his or her authority to achieve sexual gratification, it is sexual abuse. When boys do not tell about sexual abuse by women, it's because society often does not define it as abuse. This double standard leaves boys tragically silent.

As we have seen in this chapter, abusers take advantage of children's natural curiosity about sex and their naïveté about inappropriate touching. They desensitize the child to physical contact and slowly blur the boundaries between appropriate and inappropriate touches. Another purpose of touching the child in increments is to test for a reaction, and if no overt resistance is observed, the molestation continues. Here, Leon, the abuser interviewed by Douglas Pryor, describes testing his stepdaughter's reaction to his caressing: "I would keep moving my hand in between her legs... I kept telling myself, 'If she says no, I'll stop and won't do it again.' I don't know if that was true... because... she never did say 'Stop.'"[7]

In the next chapter we will suggest how parents can teach their children that inappropriate sexual touching is wrong while simultaneously nurturing their children's healthy sexual development.

Chapter 6

HOW TO TALK TO KIDS ABOUT SEXUAL DEVELOPMENT AND BODY SAFETY

This chapter will illustrate some ways that parents can teach their children how to recognize and respond to inappropriate touches while simultaneously promoting their children's healthy sexual development. As you will see, these two topics go hand in hand, and both are very important for reducing children's vulnerability to sexual abuse.

Healthy sexuality is an important part of both physical and mental health. Just as parents encourage children's cognitive, physical, emotional, and language development, it is also important for parents to nurture their children's sexual development. In the first part of this chapter, we describe children's sexual development and suggest ways parents can engage their children in discussions about sexual issues. We offer ways to

- give children accurate information about sexual development;
- answer their questions about sexuality; and
- provide sexual abuse prevention education within the context of nurturing children's sexual development.

TYPICAL CHILDHOOD SEXUAL DEVELOPMENT

The following section outlines normal sexual development for children of different ages, in terms of both sexual knowledge and behavior.[1]

Infants and Toddlers—Birth to Two Years

Baby boys have erections throughout the day and night. Some infant boys experience erections simply by stretching or coughing or during diaper changes. All babies explore their bodies. They touch their genitals just like they explore their ears and toes. They quickly learn that touching their genitals feels good. This is a natural and normal part of their development. Many kids, especially toddlers, are naturally uninhibited and often enjoy being naked.

Preschool-age Children—Three to Five Years

By the time they are two or three years old, most children know whether they are boys or girls. They define gender primarily on the basis of physical characteristics (for example, clothing or hair). This awareness is called gender identity. However, they do not understand that they will always be that gender. You might hear a three-year-old boy say he's going to grow up to be a mommy. Or if children see a picture of a boy with long hair, who is dressed in girls' clothes, they may believe that the boy has become a girl. Between the ages of five and seven, most children begin to understand that they will always be either a boy or a girl (meaning they have achieved gender constancy). Some children at this age have interests more typical of the other sex. Young boys may play with dolls, pretend to be princesses or dress up in glittery princess clothes, or even express a desire to be a girl. Girls may insist on wearing boys' clothing, may refuse to assume female characters in play-acting, and may enjoy being mistaken for a boy. These are called gender-variant behaviors and interests. Children with a gender-variant pattern may express the desire to be the other sex or claim that they really are the other sex. If your child exhibits these types of behaviors or repeatedly makes disparaging statements about his or her body parts, or talks about wanting to be the other sex, you might want to consult with someone who specializes in gender variance. The national organization of Parents, Families, and Friends of Lesbians and Gays (PFLAG) has a Transgender Network and can help you find experts.

Between the ages of three and five, children believe the sexual body parts are used for elimination; few are aware of their sexual functions. If they do mention any sexual function for genitals, their responses are primarily related to pregnancy and birth, such as "You make babies with it." They often show their genitals to other children or adults and are interested in looking at other people's bodies. Preschoolers may experiment by sticking their fingers or other objects in their own vagina or anus. Usually this hurts, and they stop doing it.

Preschoolers are also very curious about the bodies of other children. Their curiosity comes out in games like "You show me yours; I'll show you mine" or "playing doctor." When kids "play doctor" (involving same- and opposite-sex children of about the same age), they may look at each other's genitals, and this is a great opportunity to teach boundaries and remind children to play with their clothes on.

Most kids this age also touch their own genitals. Such self-touching is common during this time. Usually after age three, children are old enough to understand that even though it feels good, touching one's own genitals should be done in private.

Why do children touch their genitals? Children fondle their genitals for two primary reasons: (1) it feels good, and (2) like thumb sucking, it is self-comforting and relieves tension. Self-stimulation is a healthy, normal part of sexual development, and it is one way that children learn about and appreciate their bodies. Masturbation is not evil or harmful, as children were once told. Genital stimulation is problematic only if a child seems preoccupied with it to the exclusion of other activities, persists in doing it in public, or cannot be redirected to another activity. As you will learn in chapter 9, excessive and compulsive self-stimulation is often seen among children who have been sexually abused.

Children this age ask endless questions about everything, including questions about physical differences between boys and girls, where babies come from, and pregnancy and birth. They frequently want to touch a parent's genitals or breasts. In contrast, they rarely exhibit adultlike sexual behaviors (for example, putting their mouths on others' sex parts, French kissing, asking to engage in sexual acts, imitating intercourse, masturbating with objects, or repeatedly inserting objects into their own vaginas or anuses or into dolls or animals). Other uncommon behaviors of a child this age include trying to insert an object into another child's genitals, putting his or her mouth on a doll's genital area, or asking to be touched or stimulated in his or her genital area. It's also rare for young children to talk about sexual acts or use sexually explicit language.

School-age Children—Six to Twelve Years

School-age children have a more developed understanding about and interest in sexuality. At this age, children are quite curious about the physiology of sex and they desire concrete information about sexuality. They ask questions about pregnancy, sexual behavior, and menstruation. Debra Haffner, an authority in sexuality education, recommends introducing children to the concept of intercourse sometime between ages five and eight.[2] By age ten, about half of school-age children have some knowledge about sexual intercourse, sexual touching, and masturbation. Genital stimulation is still common and occurs at home or other private places but rarely in public. Contact experiences with other children are very common at this age. Such contact usually occurs during games with same-age peers. This contact includes kissing, hugging, fondling, exhibitionism, and role-playing. Adultlike or aggressive sexual behaviors are rare.

Preteens (10–12 years) worry a lot about whether they are normal. Boys worry about their penis size and girls worry about breast size and body image. This age is when they need to learn about menstruation, wet dreams, and other signs of pubescence. Ideally, both girls and boys should start receiving information about puberty around age eight. Since most schools do not introduce formal sex education until the fifth or sixth grade, it is important that parents provide information about puberty before children receive it in the classroom. Preteens are ready to learn about sex and reproduction. It is also important for them to know about sexually transmitted infections, birth control, and the consequences of teen pregnancy.

Adolescence—13 to 18 Years

Developing a sense of oneself as a sexual being is an important task of adolescence. Adolescents have a more adultlike understanding of sexual matters. Their questions focus on concerns about decision making, dating, sexual relationships, and sexual orientation. Conversations with teens should include messages about the responsibilities and consequences of sexual activity. Now is when it is appropriate to discuss ways to prevent date rape, unintended pregnancy, and HIV and other sexually transmitted diseases. Teenagers are also ready for discussions about consent and exploitation.

"My parents never talk to me about S-E-X—all they talk about is S-A-Ts."

During pubescence, adolescents also experience a flood of hormones. It is normal for youths this age to have sexual desires and to be curious about sexual behaviors. For many adolescents, their first sexual experiences take place alone. Masturbation is common, especially among boys. Some youths experiment with other adolescents, trying out such behaviors as open-mouth kissing, petting, and oral sex. One-half of high school students in the U.S. report having had sexual intercourse, and 17 is the median age for first intercourse.[3] Oral sex is now more common than intercourse, with 55 percent of teenagers aged 15 to 19 saying they have engaged in heterosexual oral sex.[4] It is uncommon for adolescents to be sexually interested in young children or to have sexual fantasies involving young children.

GUIDELINES FOR TALKING WITH CHILDREN ABOUT SEXUALITY

Teach Children the Correct Names for Their Genitals

The best (and often easiest) place to start your sexuality education is by teaching children the correct names for their genitals. It's important for children to know the correct terms for their genitals for several reasons. First, knowing the proper terms might make a child less vulnerable to sexual abuse. As an abuser told an interviewer for the *Rocky Mountain News*, "If children knew what different body parts were and used the correct terms, I left them alone."[5] When children use slang or "cute" nicknames for their genitals (like daisy, cookie, muffin, monkey, or dingdong), it could mean they are not being educated at home about sexuality and abusers might take advantage of children's ignorance and offer to "teach" them about sex. Second, without proper terminology, children have a hard time telling someone about sexual touching. For example, if a child reports that someone touched her "cookie" (the term used in her home for vulva), it would be difficult for the listener to recognize the disclosure of sexual abuse. Third, teaching children the correct names for all the parts of their bodies, including their genitals, helps children develop a healthy, more positive body image. In contrast, using nicknames for genitals can give children the idea that there is something shameful or bad about their genitals. This knowledge also gives children the correct language for understanding their bodies and for asking questions about their sexual development.

As soon as children start talking, they can learn to say the names of all their body parts, including the genitals. When teaching children the names of their genitals, use the correct terms: penis, testicles, scrotum, vagina, vulva, breasts, buttocks, and anus/rectum. For young children, it is usually sufficient to use the words vulva, vagina, penis, buttocks (or butt for short), and breasts. Bathing and toileting are excellent times to teach children proper terms—"Did you wash your penis?" Another way to teach the names is to sit with your child and look at picture books illustrating how boys' and girls' bodies are different. Anatomically correct dolls provide another way to introduce all the parts of the body. Many excellent picture books are available in bookstores and libraries. (For a list of books, see appendix 2.) You can teach your children these correct terms but then collectively refer to the genitals as "private parts."

You might say to a young child, "Your body is made up of many different parts. Certain special parts of your body are private. 'Private' means that no one is allowed to touch or look at these special body parts. Everybody has private parts. We cover them up to keep them private because they're so special. So private parts are the special parts of your body that are covered up by your swimsuit or underwear."[6]

OFF LIMITS SAFETY TIP #15:

Teach children the "Boss of My Body" concept.

While teaching children the correct names of their body parts, you can also introduce the concept of "body-safety empowerment," or being in charge of keeping your own body safe. Many parents have successfully taught their children the concept of being the "Boss of My Body" as a way to empower their children.[7] You can introduce children to being the bosses of their bodies in the following way. Explain to a child that because teachers are the bosses (in charge) at school, they have rules that help keep children safe at school. Then review some school safety rules, like not running in the halls, or the tried-and-true "Never run with scissors." After asking a child, "Who's the boss at home?" explain that because parents are the bosses at home, they have rules to keep children safe at home. Review some of your home safety rules, like not playing with matches or opening the door to strangers. Then you can ask the most important question: "Who's the boss of your body?" or "Who's in charge of your body?" Most children will proudly assert, "I am!" A few children may answer, "Mommy is." If they do, you can reinforce the rule that "Mommy is the boss of her own body, and you're the boss of your body." Body ownership is one of the most valuable safety lessons you can teach your child. Children who understand that their bodies belong to them and that no one else has the right to touch or look at their private parts are children who will be less vulnerable to sexual abuse. Although you wouldn't want to use the phrase "boss of my body" with older children or teenagers, the message is the same. Teenagers with a healthy concept of body ownership appreciate their own bodies. They also take responsibility for keeping themselves safe in many situations, for protecting their sexual and reproductive health, and for avoiding sexual behaviors that are harmful to themselves or others.

Start Early

As soon as children are old enough to ask questions about sex, they are old enough for answers. For some children, this can be as early as two years of age.

Don't Wait for Your Child to Start the Conversation

Many parents delay talking to their children about sexuality because their children haven't asked about it. Some children are reluctant to ask about sexuality issues; others simply don't ask a lot of questions. Your child may never ask, but he or she still needs to know. It's a parent's responsibility to introduce the topic, little by little, and to do it frequently.

Do It Often

A one-time conversation with children about sexual development is not enough. Sexuality education is an ongoing process. You don't just teach the rule—"Look both ways before crossing the street"—once. The more frequently you discuss these topics at home, the easier it will become to do so.

Be Honest

Children deserve honest and straightforward answers and explanations about sexuality and body safety. Many parents feel awkward discussing sexuality with their children, often because their own parents didn't talk to them about these issues, so they lack good role models. It's okay to feel uncomfortable. Just explain your discomfort to your child, perhaps by saying, "I'm uncomfortable talking about sex because my parents never talked with me about it. But I want us to be able to talk about anything, including sex, so please come to me if you have any questions." If you are uncomfortable talking about sexuality with your children, practice with your partner or a good friend first. If you still feel awkward discussing this topic, you might ask someone else to take the lead, which will allow you and your child to participate in the conversation.

Be Brief

When young children ask questions that might be about sexuality, clarify what they are asking, and give them no more or less information than they can understand or need to satisfy their curiosity. Stay away from long lectures. Be brief, but honest, with your answers. When James asked his dad where he had come from, his dad launched into "the talk." After 20 minutes of getting an elaborate description of intercourse, pregnancy, and childbirth, James said to his dad, "That's great, Dad. But in school today we were talking about where we were born, and Mark said he was from Chicago. I was wondering where I came from." Oops! If James's dad had clarified what he was asking ("What do you mean?") or asked James what he already knew about the subject, he might have been able to answer James's real question.

Respond Positively to Children's Questions

Young children often ask questions about how babies are made, how birth occurs, and what the physical differences are between boys and girls. These questions present a "golden opportunity" to promote healthy sexuality. Reward your children for asking such questions. Instead of asking, "Why do you want to know?" or changing the subject, praise your child for asking ("I'm so glad you asked me that!"). Be an "askable" parent. If you don't know the answer to a particular question, admit you don't know. Don't make up an answer. Explain to your child that you'll get back to him with the answer, or better yet, look the information up together (in books or on the Internet). (See appendix 2 for a description of books and videos about sexuality that parents can discuss with their children.)

"If you must know, Jimmy, you came from a box in front of the market. It said 'Free Kittens.'"

Here are some sample responses to questions about reproduction:

Question: "How are babies made?" "Where do babies come from?" "How does the baby get inside the mommy?"

Answer: "When a man and a woman love each other and want to make a baby, they get close to one another, and a tiny thing called a sperm goes from the daddy's body into the mommy's body and meets a tiny egg that was growing inside the mommy. The sperm and the egg join together and the baby grows from that. When it's big enough, the baby comes out of the mommy's body."

For an older child (between five and eight) who asks this question, you might say: "When a man and woman love each other and want to make a baby, the man and woman hug and kiss and get very close to each other. The man puts his penis inside the woman's vagina, and things called sperm come out of the man's penis and travel up the woman's vagina to her uterus. Sometimes one of those sperm and an egg that was inside the woman join together inside the woman and grow until they form a baby human being. The baby grows inside the mother's uterus for nine months, and then the baby is born." (Note: There are many ways babies are conceived other than through heterosexual intercourse. If your situation calls for a different explanation than the one provided, we encourage you to talk about it honestly with your child.)

Question: "Where does a baby grow inside the mommy?"

Answer: "In a special place just for babies called a uterus."

Question: "How does the baby get out?"

Answer: "Babies usually come out of a woman's body through an opening called a vagina." (If you choose to describe to your child how birth happens via cesarean section, you might say, "Sometimes the baby can't easily fit through the mother's vagina, so the doctor makes an opening in the mommy's belly, and then the baby comes out of her belly.")

Question: "Does it hurt the mommy when the baby comes out?"

Answer: One way to answer this question is, "It hurts for a little while, but then the baby is born and all the hurt goes away."

Now it is your turn to respond to children's questions. Imagine your son asking these questions: "Mommy, where's your penis? Can we buy you one?" How would you respond?

Or imagine your daughter asking: "Mommy, why are your nipples so much bigger than mine?" or "Mommy, why do you have hair down there?" or "Daddy, is that your tail?" How would you respond?

Young children tend to ask these kinds of questions. Older children's questions reflect their more advanced thinking and knowledge about sexuality. For example, they might ask about pregnancy, contraception, AIDS, wet dreams, menstruation, sexual orientation, and their own changing bodies.

TAKE ADVANTAGE OF TEACHABLE MOMENTS

A "teachable moment" is a natural learning opportunity for adults to discuss sexuality and body safety with children. Many situations happen during a child's or teenager's day that provide wonderful learning opportunities.

When responding to teachable moments, give children the message that you welcome all of their questions. Strive to be an "askable" parent. You can demonstrate this openness by using a nonshaming, calm, and welcoming tone of voice. You can also welcome their questions by saying something like "I'm so glad you asked" or "That's a great question. Let's talk about it." Then you can respond with basic but honest information that will satisfy their curiosity. These spontaneous moments can lead to natural discussions about sexuality and body safety and give you opportunities to teach body-safety rules.

TEACHING CHILDREN ABOUT BODY SAFETY

Without being taught, few young children naturally know that it's wrong for other people to touch or look at their genitals. As one sexually abused child said, "I didn't know there was anything wrong with it. I didn't know it was abuse. I thought he was showing me affection."[8] Here's an example of how a child was involved in a sexually abusive situation that might have been prevented if she had been taught that sexual touching was wrong:

Four-year-old Rosa loved going to her grandmother's house to play. Rosa's uncle lived with her grandmother, and he often joined her while she played with her dolls. One day he asked if he could touch her "pee-pee." That night, after she had returned to her own home, she mentioned to her mother that her uncle touched her "pee-pee" while they were playing with dolls. Her mother became upset, sent her to the bathroom to take a bath, and admonished her for letting her uncle touch her "down there." Rosa sat in the bathtub, feeling ashamed and confused, as she did not know it was wrong for her uncle to touch her private parts.

What's the best way to teach children—especially children as young as Rosa—that it is wrong for other people to touch their genitals? We recommend teaching them the difference between "OK" and "Not OK" touches of their genitals. First, explain the times when it will be OK for another person to touch their private parts. For young children who need help during bathing and toileting, say, "If you need help cleaning your private parts after you go to the bathroom or while you're taking a bath, it's OK for me (and list other caregivers) to help you clean your private parts." Also explain "When your private parts are hurt or sick, a doctor or nurse may need to touch or look at your private parts, to help you get better."[9] Reassure children that you will be with them during the exam if this may happen. With older children or teenagers, acceptable touching of the private parts occurs during routine well-child visits and gynecological and sexual-health examinations.

OFF LIMITS SAFETY TIP #16:

Teach children body-safety rules.

Once your children understand when it is appropriate and safe for another person to touch or view their private parts, then they are ready to learn some body-safety rules to keep their private parts safe, should anyone try to touch them inappropriately. These body-safety rules are just like other safety rules that you enforce, like wearing helmets while biking, or seat belts while riding in a car. We recommend teaching young children a rule to protect their private parts using "OK" and "Not OK" terms instead of teaching children the difference between "good touches" and "bad touches." The problem with the good touch/bad touch approach is that some touches that feel bad (like getting a shot or having medicine put on a cut) are actually "OK," and some touches that feel good may be "Not OK." For example, when a child's genitals are fondled, it can feel good even though it's "Not OK." Children should not be expected to decide whether a pleasurable touch is "OK" or "Not OK." Make it very easy for your child to understand. Establish a rule that says that (except for medical or hygienic reasons) adults, teenagers, or older children may not touch or look at their private parts.

Following are some body-safety rules written for both kids and teenagers. The younger the child (either mentally or chronologically), the more concrete the rule should be. Older children (ages 11–17) also need guidance, albeit in the form of safety principles. When teaching body-safety rules to older children, you can use more abstract concepts (like "consent" or "exploitation") and guidelines (such as "Trust your intuition" or "Set sexual boundaries"). Start teaching body-safety rules as soon as children can understand basic rules and are capable of having a simple understanding of right and wrong (usually by age two or three). Teach these rules as often as you can. Children learn best through practice and repetition. Learning about the protection of one's body is a process that occurs over a long period of time. It's also a good idea to have all authority figures in the family teach and practice these rules with children. When older siblings teach body-safety rules to younger siblings, it can serve as a deterrent for sibling sexual abuse.

BODY-SAFETY RULE #1
No One Is Allowed to Touch Your Private Parts

Kid language: "No one is allowed to touch your private parts, unless you need help cleaning them, or your private parts are hurt or sick and the doctor or nurse needs to examine them." (Remind children that you will be with them during doctor visits.) For parents who want to address masturbation or self-touching, you can follow this rule with "Nobody but you can touch your private parts. Since you're the Boss of Your Body, it's always OK for you to touch and look at your own private parts, as long as you do it in private, when no one else is around."

Teen language: "No one has the right to touch the private areas of your body without your permission. No one has the right to force, coerce, bribe, threaten, or manipulate you into engaging in any type of sexual activity."

BODY-SAFETY RULE #2

You Should Not Touch Someone Else's Private Parts

Kid language: "You should not touch someone else's private parts."

Teen language: "You do not have the right to touch someone else's body without that person's permission. It is never acceptable to force, coerce, bribe, threaten, or manipulate another person into any type of sexual activity." Explain to your teen that it is wrong (and a crime) to force or trick anyone, including a child, into sexual activity.

In her book, *Protecting Your Children from Sexual Predators*, Leigh Baker stresses the need to inform children and teenagers about legal ramifications of sexually abusive behaviors. She quotes one juvenile abuser who described his astonishment after learning about the seriousness of his actions: "I knew what I was doing to my sister was wrong, and that my mother would be very angry at me if she found out. But I thought that getting in deep trouble with my mom would be the most that would happen. I never knew that I could get in trouble with the law for what I did."[10]

BODY-SAFETY RULE #3

No One Is Allowed to Take Pictures of Your Private Parts

Kid language: "No one is allowed to take pictures or videos of your private parts or of you doing anything when you're naked (for example, going to the bathroom, dressing, bathing)." This body-safety rule is not meant to stop parents from taking photos of their naked children, like the cute "bathtub" photo you send to their grandparents, but to prevent someone from using children for pornographic purposes.

Teen language: "It's a crime for an adult to take pictures or videos of your naked body. If an adult offers to take pictures of you naked, refuse and tell a parent or trusted adult about this offer." Be sure your teen knows that "sexting"—sending a nude photo via cell phone—is illegal.

The next three body-safety rules teach children what to do if anyone tries to sexually abuse them. The safety skills include (1) verbally refusing (say "No"), (2) trying to get away from the person, and (3) telling a trusted adult about what happened. Rule #4 also emphasizes that it is never a child's fault if somebody tries to touch or look at his or her private parts. "Not OK" touching is always the responsibility of the abuser. According to research, most children from age three on can learn the "No, Go, Tell" body-safety skills.[11] These body-safety rules can empower children to protect themselves. Author Carla van Dam describes how children who used these body-safety skills (who said "No" and then told an adult) played a role in the arrest and conviction of some of the abusers she interviewed for her book.[12] Other abusers have said that they avoid children who refuse their requests or insist on telling their parents.[13]

BODY-SAFETY RULE #4
If Somebody Tries to Touch Your Private Parts, Say "No!"

Kid language: "If somebody tries to touch your private parts, say, 'No!' or 'Stop it!' or 'That's wrong!' or 'That's against the rules!' With most children above the age of seven, you can phrase the rule as "Say 'No' to anyone who tries to break one of your body-safety rules." Emphasize that even if they can't or don't say no, it is never their fault (or they will not be blamed or punished).

Teen language: "You have the right to refuse any sexual request made of you. Even if you cannot stop the person, it is never your fault. Abuse is always the responsibility of the abuser."

BODY-SAFETY RULE #5
If Someone Tries to Touch Your Private Parts, Try to Get Away and Tell

Kid language: "If someone tries to touch your private parts, try to get away from that person, and most importantly, tell someone else what happened, even if the person who tried to touch you tells you to keep it a secret."

Teen language: "If someone attempts to or does touch your body in an uncomfortable or inappropriate way, try to get away and then tell a trusted adult."

Help children create a list of names or categories of people (teachers, counselors) they could talk to about their concerns. Children need to know that it's okay with you that they talk to any person on their "safe adults" list. Children are sometimes reluctant to tell parents because they don't want to upset them, so telling another adult may be easier. Also, stress that they keep telling an adult until the abuser stops breaking the body-safety rule. As you will learn in chapter 9, unfortunately adults don't always believe children's disclosures, so it's important to encourage children to keep telling until someone listens and the abuse stops. Also explain to children that even if somebody touched their private parts before, and they didn't tell anyone about it, they should still tell an adult about it now. Children need to know that it's never too late to tell.

BODY-SAFETY RULE #6
Never Keep Secrets about Sexual Touching

Kid language: "Never keep secrets about someone touching your private parts. Always tell me (or any adult you trust) if anyone tries to break one of your body-safety rules, especially if they tell you to keep it a secret or they say, 'Don't tell your parents.' Even if the person says, 'I'll hurt your puppy if you tell,' you should still tell." (An alarm should go off in the child's head whenever there's a request for secrecy.)

Teen language: "If someone tells you to keep a secret about sexual touching or anything that worries, frightens, or upsets you, don't keep the secret. Even if the person threatens you or your family, talk about it with a trusted adult."

This next body-safety rule serves to protect your child from exposure to pornography. As described in chapter 4, abusers sometimes use pornography to seduce children. The abuser might show the child pictures or videos of other children performing sexual acts and then persuade the child that such activities are fun, are normal, or will make them feel good. It's important to teach children a body-safety rule about others showing them sexual or pornographic material. Be sure to use language that fits your style and the age of your child. You might prefer to call the material "dirty," "inappropriate," or "porn."

You have also learned that sexual abusers often sexualize the relationship through "sex talk"—asking a teen questions about his or her sexual activities, describing his own sexual experiences to the child, or telling the child sex jokes. An older person talking to a child or teen about sex is a major red flag. Youths need to know that this topic is not acceptable conversation.

BODY-SAFETY RULE #7
It's Not OK to Look at Pictures of Naked People

Kid language: "It's not OK for you to look at pictures or movies of people who are naked. If an older person (teenager or adult) tries to show you pictures or movies of naked people (kids or adults), say, 'No,' and tell a parent or trusted adult about it."

Teen language: "It's illegal for adults to show you pornography. If an adult tries to show you this kind of material, refuse, and tell a parent or trusted adult about it. It's never OK for an adult to speak sexually to you or tell you sexual jokes."

OFF LIMITS SAFETY TIP #17:

Practice body-safety rules by playing "What if?" games.

Playing "What if?" games is an excellent way to teach children and teens to think about and plan for experiences they may encounter in life. By posing a hypothetical scenario, you can help children learn and apply their body-safety rules and explore ways to handle potentially dangerous encounters. When you practice safety skills by using "What if?" scenarios, it can teach children to be assertive and to protect themselves should they ever be in an unsafe situation. "What if?" games are also an excellent teaching tool for helping children to build decision-making skills. Play "What if?" games as often as you can. This reinforces the skills you have taught your children and helps them to be better prepared, in case they have any unsafe encounters.

You can play "What if?" games anywhere: in the car, while shopping, or even during dinner. Get children involved in each story by asking them what they would say and do in each situation. Children love to pretend and role-play, so have them act out the scene if they want to. Although the situations you will be practicing are serious, you can make learning fun. You can pose "What if?" scenarios to teens as well; your conversations have the potential to lead into other areas of concerns to the teens.

Below are some "What if?" situations about different areas of safety. The stories include children of different ages. Choose scenarios that are most appropriate for the ages of your children. Offenders include youths and adults who have many different kinds of relationships with children. Choose people and settings most relevant to your child. Once you have explored the stories, you can make up your own. Or better yet, let your children come up with their own "What ifs?" Children often like to make up their own stories, and by doing so, they will come up with issues of concern to them. You may be surprised by how much you will learn about your children when they come up with a "What if?" story on their own. You can also pretend you do not know the answers and make mistakes when answering their questions. Kids love to teach their parents the correct answer!

For each "What if?" situation, you want a child to

- recognize that the situation is unsafe (or that a body-safety rule has been broken or that the request is inappropriate);

- know to say, "No," "Stop it," "I don't want to," "That's wrong," or "I need to check with my Mom/Dad first";
- know to try to get away from the person;
- know to tell a trusted adult (even if the child has been told to keep it a secret); and
- know that he or she is not at fault for the abuser's actions.

"What If?" Situations

1. What if you're in the bathroom at school and an older kid tries to touch your private parts? What would you say to the kid? What would you do? Would you tell anybody about what the kid did? Who could you tell? What would you tell that person?

2. What if your babysitter tells you that you can stay up late if you take a bath with him? What would you say and do? Would you tell anybody? What would you tell that person?

3. What if you go into a neighbor's house that your parents have told you not to go into, and while visiting, the neighbor tries to touch your private parts? What would you say to the neighbor? What should you do next? Would you tell anyone? (In this situation, the child disobeyed the parent by going into the neighbor's house. Recognize how difficult it would be for your child to tell you what happened, because it requires admitting to the disobedience.) Whose fault is it?

4. What if someone you didn't know very well wanted to take pictures of your private parts, saying you could become a famous model? What could you say to the person? What would you do? Would you tell anyone?

5. What if an older kid you know invites you to play a game where you pretend he or she is the doctor and you are the patient? The kid tells you to take off all your clothes so that the "doctor" can examine the "patient." What would you do? What could you say? Would you tell anybody?

6. What if your teacher says he will give you straight As if he can touch your private parts? What can you say to your teacher? What would you do? Would you tell anyone that your teacher said this? Who's to blame?

7. What if you are spending the night at your grandparents' house, and while you are sitting on the couch, your grandfather tries to touch your private parts? What can you say to him? What would you do? Would you tell anyone? Who?

8. What if you are visiting your best friend at his house and his stepfather wants to show you photographs of adults and kids with their clothes off? What can you say to him? What would you do? Would you tell anyone? Whose fault is it?

9. What if your teenage babysitter asks you to play the "I'll show you mine if you show me yours" game? What can you say to her? What would you do? What if she tells you to keep it a secret? Would you tell anyone?

10. What if your uncle, who is staying at your house, walks around naked and wants you to touch his private parts while he's watching TV? What would you say to him? What would you do? Would you tell anyone? Who? What would you say to the person you told?

OFF LIMITS SAFETY TIP #18:

Take advantage of "teachable moments" to discuss sexual development and body safety.

Let's look at some examples of "teachable moments," both for sexual development and for body-safety examples.

> *A four-year-old walks into the bathroom while her father is urinating and says, "Daddy, is that your tail?" This is a perfect opportunity to educate her about sexuality and also to teach her a body-safety rule by saying, "No, sweetie, that's not my tail. It is my penis. I have a penis because I am a man. Boys and men have penises; girls and women have vulvas on the outside and vaginas on the inside. Remember, your vulva and vagina are private and belong only to you. No one is allowed to touch your vulva or your vagina, because they're yours."*
>
> •
>
> *You and your three-year-old son are at the grocery store when you notice he is sitting in the shopping cart with his hand in his pants. If your child fondles his genitals in public places, it is important to label the behavior not as bad, but instead as inappropriate for the time or place. You can say, "Isaac, I see you're holding your penis. It's all right to touch your penis, but*

not in places where other people can see you. If you want to do that, you can do it in private when you're alone, like in your bedroom." If your son has a habit of frequently touching his penis, provide him with something else to do with his hands. If it happens while grocery shopping, then give him something else to hold, like a favorite toy or the shopping list.

•

Your eight-year-old boy-and-girl twins find Mom's tampons and ask what they are. Some parents wonder if their sons really need to know about menstruation. But both girls and boys need to know about menstruation and the mechanics of sanitary protection. You can say, "Once a month a woman bleeds from her vagina. The monthly bleeding is called menstruation. A woman puts a tampon inside her vagina to prevent the blood from getting on her clothes. Tampons are used only by grown-up women. It is never safe for children to put anything inside their private parts." If your child is ready, this is an excellent opportunity to discuss reproduction and puberty.

•

Your nine year-old son asks, "Dad, what's sex?" After finding out what your son thinks sex is, you can say, "Thanks for asking, that's a great question! Sex is when two adults who love each other agree to touch each other's private parts. Sex is for adults only, though, not children." This question presents another "golden opportunity" to start a dialogue with your son about healthy sexuality. You can start giving him the message that sexual activity should only occur between consenting adults and that sexual activity between an adult or teenager and younger children is wrong and is actually harmful and illegal.

•

Your child comes into your bedroom unexpectedly in the night while you and your partner are making love. You thought the door was locked, but it wasn't. You realize your child has been standing in your room for several minutes. How would you handle this potentially awkward moment? You can gently ask your child to leave. "We would like our privacy right now. Please go back to bed. One of us will come talk to you in a few minutes." Then go talk to your child, ask what she/he saw, and reassure your child that you are willing to answer any questions. To explain lovemaking, you can say, "When grown-ups love each other, they share their love in a special way by touching each other's private parts." (Message: This is adult behavior.) Children's responses and the questions they ask depend on their age. A four-year-old may be concerned that you were hurting each other based on the sounds heard. A young child might think you're mad at her for interrupting your privacy. "No, I'm not mad at you, but sometimes grown-ups want to be alone. When our bedroom door is closed, that means we want privacy. Next time, please knock and wait for me to open the door, okay?" (Message: In our home, we respect each other's right to privacy.) An older child might think "it's gross" that anyone would want to do that, especially his/her parents. What is most important is that you continue to offer accurate sexual information to your child. If you have been utilizing teachable moments all along and have been talking about healthy sexuality from early ages, it is less likely that your child will have a negative reaction to seeing you making love.

•

A three-year-old child is sitting on his mom's lap watching a movie. The boy puts his hand inside his mother's shirt and squeezes her breasts. If mom does not want her child to do this, she can utilize the teachable moment by saying, "I love cuddling with you, but these are my breasts and they belong to me. Please don't touch them. Remember, it's not OK to touch other people's private parts, and no one is allowed to touch your private parts, unless you need help cleaning them, or unless your private parts are hurt or sick and the doctor or nurse needs to examine them."

•

You are entertaining friends when your three-year-old daughter comes running through the living room naked. Although the other parents laugh at her behavior, you want to teach her about modesty without making her feel that her nudity is "naughty." You might say, "Now that you're a big girl, you need to cover up. These are special parts of your body that are not for everyone to see. When we have guests over, you need to keep your clothes on."

•

A four-year-old neighborhood friend (a boy) is visiting your daughter (also four) and they're playing together in her bedroom. What can you do if you walk into your daughter's bedroom and discover the two friends "playing doctor"—examining each other's bodies, including their private parts? First, try to stay calm. Getting upset will only confuse or frighten the children. Then tell them to get dressed and redirect their play. You can utilize this teachable moment by acknowledging their curiosity about body parts, but also reminding the children about their body-safety rules. You can say, "It looks like you two were playing a game and looking at each other's private parts. Let's talk about our body-safety rules. Remember, children need to keep their private parts covered up while playing games. It's OK if you want to pretend to play doctor with your clothes on, but not with your clothes off." After reviewing body-safety rules with the children, you can direct their attention to some other activity. It would also be important to inform the parent of the other child about this teachable moment. Since most sex play at this age is motivated by curiosity about what genitals look like, now is the time to talk with your children and show them picture books to help them understand the physical differences between boys and girls. (A list of these resources is in appendix 2.)

•

Your son and daughter, ages three and five, are bathing together. Your daughter is giggling and grabbing her brother's penis. He is giggling along with her. You can say to both children, "Remember, it's not OK to touch other people's private parts. You can touch your own, if you want to when you're alone, but it's not OK to touch each other's private parts."

•

You're driving with your teenage son when the two of you hear a news report on the radio of a male schoolteacher being arrested for sexually abusing a female student. You can use this news report as an opportunity to discuss sexual violations against children and teens and ask what your son's thoughts are. For example, you can ask, "What do you think about a male teacher doing this to a girl? Would you think any differently about it if a female teacher was having sex with a boy?" The purpose of this conversation would be to emphasize the inappropriateness of adults (male or female) using children and teens for sexual purposes.

•

Raising sexually healthy children is an important part of parenting. Parents are a child's first and most important teachers of sexuality. By talking to children about sexuality and responding positively to their questions, you will be giving them a solid understanding of their own sexuality. By playing "What if?" games and utilizing teachable moments, you can actively engage in body safety and sexuality education in everyday life. Through your efforts, your children are getting a head start toward becoming sexually healthy adults as well as becoming less vulnerable to sexual abuse.

Chapter 7

CHOOSING SAFE AUTHORITY FIGURES FOR YOUR CHILD

In all of the examples of childhood sexual abuse described thus far, someone has had authority over a child, was alone with that child, and took advantage of a child's natural trust and dependency, willingness to obey, desire to please, and naïveté about sexual activities. The purpose of this chapter is to offer suggestions for how to choose safe authority figures and activities for your child.

OFF LIMITS SAFETY TIP #19:

Carefully screen substitute caregivers.

Parents often have difficulty finding quality substitute care. How do you know that the person you are choosing will care for and keep your children safe? First, avoid allowing someone you just met to care for your children. Just as it takes time to find the best pediatrician or dentist for your child, it takes time to find a good sitter or nanny. Also, be aware that statistically, it is riskier to hire adolescent sitters. If you do hire teenagers, be especially careful when screening them. Here are some guidelines for choosing in-home caregivers. Even though this screening process may initially seem burdensome, it is well worth following for the safety of your children.

Check references. Ask for references from people who know the applicant (for example, relatives, friends, or neighbors), including prior child-care employers. One helpful question to ask other parents who have used the sitter is whether they would hire the person again to care for their own children. Ask them questions about the sitter's level of maturity and responsibility, and ask whether their children liked him or her. You might also ask the reference person, "What might be an area where you feel the person needs further growth and development?" Even if you know and like the parents of a prospective teenage sitter, approach hiring the teenager with full vigilance.

Do background checks. You can request a criminal or noncriminal background check on any person through your local police department, county sheriff's office, or state's Bureau of Investigation. You can also have background checks done online, for a fee (for example, at www.ussearch.com). To do so, you will need the person's full name and date of birth. A background check will tell you if the person has any criminal record, including sexual offenses. You can also check the National Sex Offender Registry (www.nsopw.gov), to see if the person has been formerly charged with child sexual assault. Several other existing Web sites can help you locate registered sex offenders (for example, www.kidsneedprotection.com, www.mapsexoffenders.com, or www.familywatchdog.us). Be aware that only sexual abusers who have been convicted show up on the registered list. Also, know that only a very small percentage of abusers are ever arrested and convicted.

Check driving records. If the sitter or nanny will be transporting your children in a vehicle, it is important to check the prospective sitter's driving record. You will want to know if the person has a record of reckless driving, driving under the influence of drugs or alcohol, speeding tickets, etc. With a name and birth date, you can obtain this information from your local department of motor vehicle office.

Conduct an interview. Getting references from others who know the applicant is necessary, but using your own judgment and intuition by conducting your own interviews is even more important. Get to know applicants by interviewing them and asking them thought-provoking questions (check out www.printablechecklists.com for a prospective babysitter checklist). When considering hiring adolescents to care for your children, you will need to get additional information. For example, ask the adolescent why he or she wants to care for children. Ask about his or her other interests. Ask what the teenager likes to do when not babysitting and what kinds of hobbies or activities the teen enjoys. Ask about the teen's friendships. Through these kinds of questions, you can determine if a teenager is involved with same-aged peers, or if his or her activities and interests focus exclusively on children. If a teen's interest in spending time with children isn't balanced with an interest in same-age relationships, then there might be a reason to be concerned. You could also meet with the teen's parents, to check out your comfort level with his/her family.

Conduct a trial run. Do a trial run with the prospective sitter. Ask the sitter to supervise your children doing some activity (playing a game, giving the dog a bath, doing a craft project), and observe how he or she interacts with your children. Then go to another part of the house and leave the sitter alone with your children. Later, ask your children if they liked the person, and take seriously any concerns they express.

Review rules and expectations. If you have decided to hire the sitter, then arrange a final meeting where you clearly discuss your expectations and rules together with your children and the sitter so that everyone understands them. Review your body-safety rules and make sure the sitter understands and supports them. Invite the sitter to be a member of your prevention team. Clearly outline what you expect the sitter to do—help with homework?—and not do—give children baths? Along with emergency telephone numbers, post your rules, which may include:

- locations in the house that may be off limits
- bathing and bedtime routines
- television and computer use (for children and sitter)
- use of alcohol, drugs, and cigarettes
- privacy during bathing, dressing, and sleeping
- children's permission to say "No" if asked to do something unsafe or to do anything else that might make the child uncomfortable
- having friends visit (for children and sitter)
- leaving the house
- driving with the children
- no secrets allowed (children have been taught that if any rules are broken, they are to tell parents)

By clearly stating your rules, you are letting this person know that yours is an off limits child and that you also have an off limits home. (See the handouts in appendix 1.)

Before you leave your child in the care of someone else, here's how you might word some of these rules: "Your (sitter, sibling, whoever) is going to care for you tonight. You all know the rules. In bed by 9 o'clock and no baths. Only watch the shows or movies we have okayed. Follow all your safety rules, and remember, we do not keep secrets in this home. Have fun. We love you, and we'll see you in the morning." Then, in the morning, ask your children how the evening went, what they did, and whether they liked the sitter. If you choose to hire this sitter again, you might drop in unexpectedly to see how your children are doing. Some parents install a nanny cam, which is a small, wireless camera that keeps a record of your children's activities. These cameras can be a good deterrent even if not turned on, because child-care workers will believe they are being monitored.

If there is anything about this sitter that makes you or your children feel uncomfortable, don't talk yourself out of your discomfort. You might discuss your concerns with the sitter or talk to your children about how they feel about this person. You also may decide not to hire that person to care for your children again. Trust your intuition and err on the side of caution.

OFF LIMITS SAFETY TIP #20:

Trust your intuition.

One of the greatest tools you possess to keep children safe is your intuition. Some people refer to it as "trusting your instincts," "listening to your gut," or "using your sixth sense." Maybe it's that nagging voice in your head that fills you with apprehension, suspicion, or worry. Safety expert Gavin de Becker calls intuition a "brilliant guardian."[1] In fact, the root of the word "intuition," *tueri*, means to guard and protect. Our intuition, or safety radar, can guide us through unsafe territory. But sometimes parents discount their "safety radar." Parents give lots of reasons for ignoring their intuition regarding their children's safety. "What if I speak up and I'm wrong? I don't want to offend her." "If I question her, she'll treat my child differently." "I'm being paranoid." "If I talk about my concerns, I could ruin his reputation." At the core of these statements and questions is often self-doubt about one's judgment. Sometimes parents are concerned about ruining someone's reputation, hurting others' feelings, or worrying about what other people might think of them. If you are ever in a situation where your "safety radar" is flashing but you're worried about hurting someone's feelings, ask yourself, "What's more important, my child's safety or the other person's feelings?" Always trust your internal warning system.

OFF LIMITS SAFETY TIP #21:

Be a questioning parent before allowing children to play or sleep at someone else's home.

Play dates and sleepovers are popular activities for preschool and school-aged children. Before you allow your child to play or sleep at someone else's home, it is important to check out the safety level of the environment. Here are some questions that parents might ask to learn more about a new playmate's home. You probably don't need to ask all of these questions every time your child visits someone else's home. Instead, select the questions that are most important to you, and use your own style of asking questions.

- What kinds of activities will the kids be doing?
- Who will be present when my child is there (for example, other family members, relatives, service people, sitters)? Will you be there the entire time or will you be leaving at any point? (One mother told us that she called an hour into her four-year-old daughter's first play date to check on her daughter. She found out that the mother who was present when she dropped her daughter off was no longer there, and the 16-year-old daughter who lived in the home was supervising the children. The mother was upset that she was not informed about the change in supervision.)
- Who will be supervising the children? Come up with agreements on supervision (for example, "I'd prefer they only play together with adult supervision").
- Are there older children or teenagers living in your home? If so, will the teens be supervising the children or will you?

• What are your rules regarding television or Internet use?

• What are the sleeping arrangements?

And although not necessarily related to sexual abuse, these last four questions are more about general safety:

• Are there any guns in the home? If so, where are they kept?

• If the kids start fighting, what do you do? (Or ask similar questions to determine how the parent disciplines children.)

• Do you have a swimming pool?

• Can the kids get access to drugs or alcohol?

Perhaps you can begin this "safety checking" process by meeting with the parent(s). You might say, "Sammy is so excited about having a new friend and coming to play at your home. For his first play date at your home, I'd like to come with him. Would that be okay with you?" Once you're there, invite the parent to discuss safety. You could say, "I am happy about Sammy's new friendship with your son. Whenever my child has a new friend, it's important to me that I get to know his friend's family, and have you get to know my family. I'm also interested in knowing each other's safety practices. Can we talk about this?" Or you could say, "When kids come to my house, here's what we do and here are the rules in my home." At this point, you could explain the safety rules in your home (no secrets; no touching each other's private parts; your kids are allowed to disobey unsafe requests; your kids have been instructed to tell you if any of their safety rules have been broken; etc.). After describing your rules, then you might ask the other parent to describe his or her rules. The purpose of this discussion is not to interrogate the parent, but to gauge the safety level of the home and to ultimately feel comfortable with the person who will be caring for your child. Pay attention to how the parent(s) responds to your questions about safety. If there is anything about the home or the parent's responses to your questions that makes you uncomfortable, trust your intuition, and make an informed decision.

How will you feel asking other parents these kinds of questions? Are you concerned that they will think you are crazy, paranoid, or overprotective? Do you worry that your child will never be invited to a friend's home again? These apprehensions may keep you from asking important questions. On the other hand, when parents inquire about their children's environments, they are able to make safer decisions for their children. It may be awkward having these discussions at first, but many parents have told us that with practice, the whole approach becomes easier and more comfortable. Practice with your friends, or with people you already know and with whom you are comfortable, before asking these questions of new acquaintances. Parents have shared stories about how they have built stronger friendships and alliances with others, just by asking these kinds of questions. Other parents have told us that they appreciate being asked these questions, because the questions show that the parent is concerned about children's safety. One mother told us about her experience being a questioning parent:

> *My daughter had a play date with a new friend from school. I decided to accompany her to her first play date, as I was interested in getting to know the family of my daughter's new friend. During that play date I discussed various issues of safety with the child's mother and asked specific questions about supervision, discipline practices, television use, and safety rules in her home. I let the mother know the safety rules in my home, as well. I was nervous that she would think I was being paranoid. Instead, she expressed appreciation that I cared enough to ask. We found a common interest in children's safety and agreed on some rules for our children when they played together. This experience has given me more confidence to ask the questions I feel are important for my child's safety. Regardless of what other people think of me, I will continue to be a questioning parent.*

OFF LIMITS SAFETY TIP #22:

Check in with children when they stay overnight at a friend's home.

When your child is spending the night at a friend's home, call and speak to her about how things are going, and ask if she's feeling comfortable staying there. Make sure your children know that they can call you at any time and that if they ever want to come home, you or someone else will come and get them right away. Parents may be reluctant to do this if it's in the middle of the night, but a child may be in an uncomfortable or unsafe situation in someone else's home and may not be able to tell you that over the phone. To be on the safe side, go pick them up anytime he or she requests it. Another option is to be the parent who has the sleepover in your home.

OFF LIMITS SAFETY TIP #23:

Be a questioning parent of administrators at your child's school, day care, faith-based institution, and youth-serving organization.

Safety in schools. Parents expect their children to be safe at school, and most of the time they are. The unfortunate reality, however, is that sexual abusers take advantage of their authority and their easy access to children in many different school settings including public or private schools, day-care centers, after-school programs, boarding schools, and residential schools (for example, treatment programs for troubled youth, or schools for hearing and visually impaired children). The inherent authority of school employees like teachers, classroom aides, counselors, and administrators makes access to and privacy with children effortless. Robert J. Shoop, author of the book *Sexual Exploitation in Schools*, says, "Many parents and many schools, even to this day, think [sexual abuse in schools] is a very unusual and very rare situation. But there are thousands of children being harmed every day by teachers and coaches in school systems."[2]

Even though the vast majority of school personnel are competent, caring, and safe people, sometimes certain individuals seek out these settings to obtain access to children and to exploit their authority by sexually abusing students or residents. Most arrests for sexual misconduct in schools are of teachers, particularly teachers who spend time alone with students giving one-on-one instruction.

To learn what a school or day-care center is doing to protect students from sexual victimization, ask questions about the institution's policies regarding sexual abuse prevention. Here are some sample questions you might ask of school/day-care administrators:

- Are criminal background checks performed on all employees and volunteers?
- Is each person checked against state and local law enforcement databases and the National Sex Offender Registry?

- Do you obtain fingerprints of all employees and volunteers?

- Do you conduct thorough screenings that involve personal interviews and reference checks? How do you screen for possible offenders?

- What kind of training do you offer to employees and volunteers about childhood sexual abuse and its prevention? Are all school employees trained to recognize warning signs that a fellow employee may be abusing children or signs that a child may be being victimized?

- Does your school or day care offer sexual abuse prevention education for children or workshops for parents? (If not, request that they do. See appendix 2 for many personal safety education programs that can be implemented in schools and day-care centers.)

- How is your environment set up to reduce the likelihood that a child could be sexually abused? Are there any secluded areas on the institution's grounds where children could be abused? For example, do the bathrooms contain areas where children can be isolated? (Two-thirds of all day-care sexual abuse takes place in bathrooms.)[3]

- What policies are in place to prevent sexual abuse of the students? For example, do you have any policies that restrict adults from being alone with a child? What do you do to make sure that children are protected when they are alone with adults? Is there adequate supervision during nap and play times?

- What are the day-care center's diaper-changing policies?

- Are parents permitted to visit without calling first? Are there any areas that are off limits to parents?

- Are all visitors screened by the office?

- Are you licensed by the state?

- Have any complaints of sexual misconduct been filed against any of your employees?

Broward County Public Schools in Florida, the nation's sixth largest school district, recently installed a visitor management system (www.siscocorp.com) to document and track visitors as they enter and exit school sites. Nicknamed the STAR (Security Tracking and Response) System, it screens visitors against the National Sex Offender Registry as well as state and local law enforcement databases. Be concerned about a program that does not employ thorough background checks; however, also be aware that fingerprinting and background checks identify only people who have been involved in the criminal justice system. The majority of people who commit sex offenses do not get caught, let alone convicted, so registries and background checks will not identify all abusers. Extend your inquiry by also finding out if and how the school trains its staff on keeping children safe from sexual abuse.

Safety in faith-based institutions. Communities of faith are places where children develop spiritually, with the support and guidance of trusted religious leaders and youth mentors. Unfortunately, no community of faith is free from the risk of child sexual abuse. As we discussed in chapter 2, people who sexually abuse children come from all class, racial, and religious backgrounds. They range from ordinary citizens to leading religious leaders.

Children are vulnerable in churches, synagogues, mosques, and other types of religious institutions for several reasons:

- Religious leaders have access to children and opportunities to be alone with them.
- Children do not question the authority of a religious leader.
- Parents trust religious leaders.

As we know from reports of sexual abuse in the Catholic Church, "decent" public presentation can cover up "deceitful" private behavior.[4] Dr. Gary Schoener, a psychologist who has counseled hundreds of clergy victims, says, "The easiest targets are the devout, because they can be conned more easily. Priests tend to inflict maximum damage on their devout victims because Catholicism teaches that priests are God's representatives on earth, worthy of complete obedience and trust. To children, it often seems as though God is abusing them, a violation that can forever destroy the refuge organized religion provides."[5]

Fortunately, more and more religious communities are using child sexual abuse prevention policies, resources, and curricula (see appendix 2). These materials teach sexual abuse prevention in a faith-based context.

You have many ways you can help protect children and youth from being sexually abused in faith communities. You might ask your faith's administrators:

- What policies have been implemented to eliminate risks of sexual violation?
- How do you screen potential volunteers and prospective employees?
- Are background checks conducted on all employees and volunteers who will be working with children and youths?
- What are the policies regarding adult supervision?
- Are there are any policies to prohibit adult-child interactions outside of faith-sponsored events? Some faith communities require that if a teen or adult advisor wishes to be in contact with a youth outside of faith-sponsored events, it must be with the knowledge and consent of the parents, and the advisor's supervisor must also be notified.
- What's being done to ensure that congregations, schools, camps, and youth events are safe places for children and young people?
- What prevention education programs are being implemented? If nothing is being done, request that such education be offered to all groups (children, youths, and adults).

You might also volunteer to be on a committee to establish a prevention program. Resources are available for children where sexual abuse prevention is taught in the context of religious beliefs and values (see appendix 2).

Safety in youth-serving organizations. Youth-serving organizations include Boy/Girl Scouts, Big Brothers Big Sisters, 4-H clubs, summer camps, recreation centers, and sporting leagues. Participating in sports, camps, and clubs is important for children's physical and social development. Many of these organizations promote close and caring relationships between youths and adults, but that same closeness can provide opportunities for abuse to occur. Some of these organizations and activities can inadvertently provide abusers with opportunities to spend private time with children and gain the trust and control needed to sexually violate them.

Here are some sample questions to ask when exploring what an organization is doing to protect youth from being sexually victimized:

- Are criminal background checks performed on all your employees and volunteers?

- Is each person checked against the National Sex Offender Registry as well as state and local law enforcement databases?

- Do you obtain fingerprints for all employees and volunteers?

- Do you ask applicants about previous histories of sexual offenses, violence against youth, and other criminal activities?

- Do you conduct thorough screenings that involve personal interviews and reference checks? (Childhood victimization expert David Finkelhor argues that organizations should, along with background checks, do "foreground checks," meaning that the topic of child protection be brought to the "fore" in recruitment and hiring. He urges organizations to inform all applicants about the importance of child protection.[6] You might want to avoid programs that do not use multiple methods to screen staff.)

- How is the environment of your organization set up to reduce the likelihood that a child could be sexually victimized?

- Do you have guidelines that cover (a) the circumstances when adults are allowed to be alone with children, (b) what kind of touching is acceptable, and (c) how toileting and other private activities are handled?

- Do you place any limits on physical contact between youths and employees during organization-sanctioned activities and programs? (Some sports such as gymnastics, cheerleading, dancing, skating, golf, and tennis pose a greater risk of boundary violations and sexual contact than others because there is more physical contact between coach and athlete.)

- Many sports require youths to change into uniforms or swimming suits. What are youth sports administrators doing to ensure safe physical and sexual boundaries in those times? For example, are there any policies about coaches accompanying youths into locker rooms while they shower?

- What training do you offer to employees and volunteers about sexual misconduct and the consequences for this inappropriate behavior? Do you have policies about sexual misconduct as part of the employee handbook?

- Are you licensed by the state? Are you accredited by an official association (for example, the American Camp Association)?
- Have any complaints of abuse ever been filed against your agency?

Here's how one father used these questions to check out a possible summer camp for his son:

> *I was considering sending my son to summer camp the year he turned eight. I had a lot of questions about safety rules and procedures at the camp. While I knew the importance of learning as much about the environment of the camp as possible, I still worried that my questions would somehow result in my son being treated differently. I worried that people would judge my parenting style and call me paranoid. Nevertheless, I met with the camp director and asked specific questions about safety for children, including their policies concerning an adult with a single child, sleeping arrangements, and sexual misconduct. The director commended me for asking difficult but necessary questions, and he was willing to discuss all of my concerns. When I requested a meeting with the counselors, they were agreeable to this, as well. Their positive responses to my need for information helped me to feel comfortable sending my son to this camp. I believe that actively inquiring about my son's safety is not only my obligation, but an invaluable message to him and to all the people in his life.*

Along with asking these types of questions, it is important for you to visit the facility (often and unannounced). It may be challenging, inconvenient, or embarrassing to inquire about your child's safety. Being a questioning parent takes extra effort, but that extra effort is what protects children.

OFF LIMITS SAFETY TIP #24:

Discuss children's safety practices with authority figures.

We recommend that you give authority figures who spend time alone with your children the following information. This includes family members, children's caregivers, school personnel, religious leaders, leaders of youth organizations, sports coaches, etc.

Off Limits Safety Practices

1. My children have been taught body-safety rules and our family regularly reviews these rules. Children's body-safety rules include not touching other people's private parts and not allowing others to touch theirs.

2. My children have been taught to obey authority figures, unless the authority figure asks them to break any of their body-safety rules or jeopardizes their safety in any way, in which case they have been given permission to say "No" to the person.

3. My children have been instructed to tell me (and other safe adults) if anyone tries to break any of their body-safety rules or asks them to do anything that worries or frightens them. Furthermore, my children and I have open communication and no topics are off limits in our home.

4. My children have been taught not to keep secrets from me.

By describing these four off limits safety practices to all authority figures, you are letting any potential abuser know that you and your children are fully equipped with body-safety knowledge, rules, and skills. You can also invite all the safe people in your children's lives to reinforce these practices when they care for your children. You're effectively placing yourself between a potential abuser and your child—acting as a safety buffer.

Here's an example of a parent describing her safety practices to her child's teacher during a parent-teacher conference. Cherise started off by asking her son's teacher questions like,

> *What academic expectations do you have for my child this year? What are your classroom rules for the kids? What are your safety rules for both inside and outside the classroom? I want to know what your safety rules are, so I can explain them to my child and make sure he understands them. I would also like you to know about our family safety rules. We expect our children to follow rules and obey authority, except in situations where doing so might jeopardize their safety. Those exceptions have to do with being asked to keep secrets or responding to any inappropriate or unsafe requests. Our kids have been taught that if someone requests that they keep a secret from their parents, they do not keep the secret*

and instead tell us right away. They have been taught that if anyone asks them to do anything that's inappropriate or unsafe, they are allowed to refuse the request. We have also taught our children body-safety rules that include rules about not touching other people's private parts and not allowing others to touch theirs. These rules are very important to us and we regularly review them at home. We tell everyone who spends time with our children about these rules, and hope that you will be part of our safety team and help us reinforce these rules at school.

This kind of conversation will let people in your child's life know that your child is educated about body safety and is off limits to any sexual activities.

Here's an example of a mother discussing her daughter's safety rules with the school's transportation director:

Mari received a brochure from the school district describing bus transportation. The brochure stated that the bus drivers' driving records were checked and that the drivers were trained in safety. One section in the brochure described students' responsibilities for keeping themselves safe—one of which was to "obey all directives" from the bus driver. Mari saw this as an opportunity to inform the director of the transportation department about her family's safety rules, including the "obey unless you feel unsafe" rule. She called the director and after expressing her pleasure at the focus on student safety, she referred to the brochure's wording about "obeying directives" by saying, "I expect my child to obey adult directives, but I do want you to know that I teach my children exceptions to that rule. My children are expected to obey adults unless the directive hurts or threatens to hurt them in any way." The director understood the need for this rule and commended Mari for giving her daughter this type of education. Mari also asked the director if the school district had any other policies aimed at preventing sexual abuse, or if the district required background checks on its bus drivers. She was reassured to learn that they did both background checks and training on identifying and reporting suspected sexual abuse. Mari was very pleased with the director's responses to her questions and felt much more comfortable placing her daughter's safety in the hands of the bus driver.

OFF LIMITS SAFETY TIP #25:

Be a questioning staff member in a school or youth-serving institution.

Staff members are in an excellent position to observe inappropriate behaviors that may indicate a fellow employee is sexually abusing children. What are those signs? They often include the following:

The person

- spends time alone with a child, either inside or outside of the school setting. (One male teacher gave a female student detention during recess and then sexually abused her in a closet in the classroom while the other children were playing outside.)
- showers a particular child with gifts or money. (A classroom paraprofessional gave an expensive birthday gift to one child.)
- initiates touching activities with a child. (A cafeteria server tickles, touches, lifts children off the ground, and hugs the kids.)
- makes sexual comments about children or teens. (One service worker was overheard saying to another, "Boy, would I like to get in her pants.")
- performs "special" favors for a child. (A bus driver drove a child all the way up to her house instead of dropping her off on the street. A female teacher drove a teenage boy to and from his basketball games.)

Reflecting on these behavioral signs, would you be concerned about Mr. Bennett, the librarian in in the following example?

The elementary-school children absolutely adore their librarian, Mr. Bennett (whom they affectionately call "Mr. B"), and in turn, he adores the children who visit his library. Still single and in his 50s, he is exceptionally skilled at encouraging children to learn to read. To encourage them, Mr. B gives gifts to the kids in his library class—candy, toys, stickers, and stuffed animals—always asking parents for permission to do so. He finds out the children's birth dates and gives them cards and presents on their birthdays. He often gives kids hugs and "high fives." During story time, Mr. B sits on the floor in the reading circle and lets the children sit on his lap while he's reading. Along with acting like a kid, he also dresses like one; his clothing always has some kind of "kid" theme, like a cartoon character. He attends the kids' sporting events on the weekends, and every school play. Quite often, Mr. Bennett asks a mother for permission to take her son with him to the city library, so together they can experience the wonders of books on a much larger scale.

Do you find Mr. Bennett's behaviors cause for concern or is he just a very child-centered employee of the school? If you were concerned about his behaviors, what might make it difficult to intervene? It's never easy to accuse a coworker of inappropriate behaviors. You might worry about ruining his or her reputation, losing a friendship, or even encountering legal problems. Many times coworkers don't know whom to talk to about their suspicions. In most youth-serving settings, it's best to report such concerns to the person's supervisor, like the director or principal. Some schools have a resource officer who is trained to receive reports concerning inappropriate or potentially criminal behaviors. Sometimes it helps to talk to a colleague in your setting, to see if he or she has noticed anything suspicious about this person. Even if your colleague disagrees with you, be sure to trust your intuition. Err on the side of children's safety and voice your concerns to the appropriate authorities.

Children can be sexually abused anytime they are alone with someone who has power and authority over them. Homes, schools, religious institutions, and youth organizations are just some of the places where a potential abuser has opportunities to be alone with a child. Does this mean you should never allow your child to spend the night at a grandparents' home or a best friend's house? Does it mean you should not let your child participate in religious or sporting activities or join youth-serving organizations? Of course not. You cannot insulate your children from the world, nor is it healthy to do so, but you can be actively involved in their lives and empower them with knowledge and skills to keep themselves safe. You can use your safety radar to make sure an abuser never gets the privacy and access he or she needs. And most importantly, by putting into practice the safety tips in this book, you can give all the people who know your child a very clear message: my child is off limits to sexual abusers!

Chapter 8

PROTECTING CHILDREN AND TEENS FROM A MODERN MENACE: ONLINE SEXUAL PREDATORS

The Internet is a wonderful resource and teaching tool for everyone—children, teens, and adults. It provides young people with exciting ways to gather information and connect with new people. Children and teens can use it to conduct school research, find helpful information, experience new cultures, and communicate with friends around the world. Cyberspace has a dark side, however. The World Wide Web contains two major risks for children: unsuitable content and unsafe contacts.

DANGERS OF INAPPROPRIATE MATERIAL

Most content found on the Internet is useful. But deviant, perverse, and violent pornography is also available. It's easy for any Internet user, including children, to be accidentally exposed to sexually explicit material. A 2007 study found that 38 percent of children who were regular Internet users had received pornographic pop-ups, 36 percent had visited a pornographic Web site by accident, and 25 percent had received pornographic material in an e-mail.[1] Just typing the word "sex" into the Google search engine brings up more than 50 million sites, many of which are pornographic. A common complaint among all Internet users is the pervasiveness of pop-up porn. Another way that accidental exposure to pornography can happen is by typing an incorrect Web site address. For example, if your son meant to type www.books.com but instead typed www.boobs.com, in one simple click of a button he would be exposed to detailed pornographic material. Here are some real examples of kids being accidentally exposed to inappropriate material:

> *Camella, a mother of four in Woodruff, South Carolina, looked at her 11-year-old daughter's Internet history and saw a string of pornographic sites and pop-ups. When she asked her daughter, Lindsay, what was going on, the girl told her mom that she had just been trying to find out what a Playboy Bunny was. "It turns out a friend was talking about Playboy Bunnies at a birthday party, and Lindsay got curious," Camella says. "She wondered if it was a toy. When I asked her about it, she said, 'Mom, I didn't want any of that stuff to come up.' She started to cry, and I knew she was scared."*[2]
>
> •
>
> *José, a 10-year-old boy from Los Angeles, really liked science. He was especially interested in viruses, particularly the Ebola virus, which he had read about in the newspaper and seen on his TV. His dad had a book about viruses called* The Hot Zone. *One morning, while using the Yahoo search engine, José typed in the words "Hot Zone" to see if he could find out more about the Ebola virus. What he found was a sexually explicit Web site complete with photographs. "Dad," Jose called out laughing, "you better come see this." Startled, José's father sat down at the computer with him and helped him to find accurate information about the Ebola virus.*[3]

Once your children begin surfing the Internet, it's important to talk to them about pornography because the risk of being exposed to it is so high. Share your views about pornography with your child. Some parents criticize pornography because it shows sex in a depersonalized way, devoid of dignity, respect, or love. Aggressive sex is portrayed as normal and exciting, and makes it seem as if there's nothing wrong with using other people (including children) in a sexual way. Both Lindsay's and José's parents had perfect teachable moments for discussing this sensitive but important topic with their children. This moment would also be a time to review Body-Safety Rule #7 with your children: "It's not okay for you to look at pictures or movies of people who are naked. If an older person (teenager or adult) tries to show you pictures or movies of naked people, say 'No,' and tell a parent or trusted adult about it." By having this discussion, you would be reminding your children about the inappropriateness of adults ever using children in these kinds of activities.

Along with accidentally coming upon pornography sites, it's also very easy to find them on purpose. Curious children and teens can easily access a variety of adult-oriented Web sites on the Internet, including pornography sites, adult video sites, and romance/dating services. Pornographic Web sites, those that involve both still photos and X-rated videos, are filled with every imaginable image and sexual act. Preteens and teenagers frequent such sites, as was the case for Chris, who sexually abused his sister Laura. Chris spent a lot of time doing online surfing of pornographic sites that contained videos of sexual acts. Several of these sites required credit card access, and charges appeared on his parents' credit card statements. His parents, however, never asked about these charges, nor monitored his online activities, talked to him about safe computer use, or installed protective software.

OFF LIMITS SAFETY TIP #26:

Install protective software on your child's computer.

Be sure your child's computer has adequate protective software installed to filter out unsuitable content and to block access to objectionable sites. Many tools are available that parents can use to guide their children to safe and rewarding online experiences. These tools can (1) filter sexually explicit graphic descriptions or images; (2) monitor children's online activities; (3) limit the amount of time your child spends online; (4) prevent a child from giving strangers personal information; and (5) filter sexual or otherwise inappropriate words or images. (Go to www.kids.getnctwise.org/tools to find the tools to fit your family's needs.)

INTERNET SEXUAL ABUSE

The Internet is an ideal way for sexual abusers to solicit sex with youths who are most commonly teenage girls between the ages of 13 and 15. The Internet provides access to countless teens in a relatively anonymous environment (the perfect opportunity for privacy). And it's not a rare event. A recent national survey found that one in eight teenagers received unwanted sexual solicitations over the Internet.[4]

Online predators solicit teenagers over the Internet in much the same way that they do in person. In one study of online predators, the majority (81 percent) found their victims in chat rooms, and one-half of them reviewed online profiles of minors (like on MySpace) to identify potential victims.[5] (MySpace, Twitter, hi5, YouTube, and Facebook are popular social-networking sites that teens use to post profiles and pictures, leave messages, and connect with new people.) When asked what they looked for in chat rooms or profiles, sexual abusers mentioned three main themes. First, they look for minors who mention sex in any fashion. For example, when a youth states in her profile that she is interested in having a good time with guys, it's an impetus for a predator to contact her. Second, online predators look for youths who appear needy, submissive, or lonely and alienated from parents and friends. One cyber predator stated, "Neediness is very apparent when a child will do anything to keep talking to you. Also, that they are always online shows a low sense of parental contact or interest in the child." Third, online predators look at screen names. If a teen uses a young-sounding or sexually provocative name (such as HOT15sweetie) or if the teen posts a provocative picture, it motivates some predators to contact those teens.

Once an online predator has selected a vulnerable teen, he begins e-mail or chat-room correspondence, often disguising certain aspects of his identity like his name, family status, or employment. The media often portrays cyber predators as adults pretending to be peers who strike up relationships with children and then lure them into encounters that tragically end in rape and/or murder. In reality, predators rarely represent themselves as teenagers. In one study, only 5 percent of offenders represented themselves online as peers.[6] Another 25 percent shaved a few years off their actual age (for example, a man who was 45 told his victim he was 35). Most Internet offenders do not deceive victims about the fact that they are adults interested in sexual relationships.

How do cyber predators engage their victims? First, they begin interacting with dialogue that is seemingly harmless. Over time (usually one to six months), the predator gains the affection, interest, and trust of the teen. As the teen begins to trust the new online friend, conversations become increasingly personal. Sometimes the correspondence advances to the exchange of gifts or pictures and to phone conversations. Although some cyber predators immediately engage in sexually explicit conversations, more often they gradually introduce sexual content into conversations and encourage sexual talk. The predator slowly introduces sexually explicit questions and comments in order to reduce the teen's inhibitions. Teenagers from age 13 to 15 are particularly vulnerable because of their growing curiosity about sex, their desire to be more grown up, their interests in forming relationships, and their needs for independence. Cyber predators exploit these vulnerabilities.

> *At age 13, Justin Berry began using his Webcam to meet friends online. He joined a popular Web site and posted his profile. He was immediately bombarded by messages from "friends" who turned out to be an online community of pedophiles, who began paying Justin to take off his clothes. At first they were "harmless" requests to take off his shirt, for $50. Then the requests got bolder, included pulling down his boxer shorts, and then they paid him to masturbate in front of the camera. Justin was slowly being transformed into an Internet porn star. In 2005, investigative reporter Kurt Eichenwald broke Justin's story with a front-page* New York Times *exposé on the dark underworld of "camkids"—children who use Webcams to produce pornography.*[7]

DANGERS OF MEETING ONLINE PREDATORS

The other danger of teens traveling alone in cyberspace is who they might meet, especially in chat rooms. Internet chat rooms are sites where individuals communicate in real time on their computers. Chat rooms have become very popular with teenagers, and also with abusers looking for victims. Cyber predators enter a chat room and strike up a relationship with a teen. Often these teens are already vulnerable kids who find it difficult to make friends face-to-face. Predators know what to say to these teens to gain their trust, meet their intimacy needs, and arouse their sexual interest. Then a predator arranges to meet the teen, with the intent of pursuing sex. Here are three teens who had such meetings:

> *Kristen, a 14-year-old star student and athlete, was seduced online by a predator nearly twice her age. Her predator traveled from Texas to California to meet and have sex with Kristen. He left her psychologically*

crippled. One day, while her parents were at church, Kristen hanged herself. Kristen's mother warns other parents that "the Internet is a sly danger" and in her daughter's honor she is trying to change the way predators operate online.[8]

•

On April 30, 2008, police arrested a 32-year-old man who was accused of luring a girl from Fullerton, California, to south Florida, where he molested her. He met the 15-year-old girl on MySpace.com and continued their relationship for about four months. The man bought the teen a plane ticket, and on April 10, he picked her up at the Fort Lauderdale–Hollywood International Airport, drove her to a nearby apartment, and raped her. Hollywood police got a tip that a missing teen might be found in the apartment, and they found the teenager inside, stripped of her personal identity, innocence, and pride. The man had allegedly promised to help the girl break into show business.[9]

•

Another teen is Alicia Kozakiewicz (we met her in chapter 1), who at age 13 was abducted outside her home in Pittsburgh by a man she met in a chat room. She was held hostage, tortured, and sexually abused for four days until the FBI rescued her. She now speaks around the country to middle school students about the dangers of online relationships, telling kids, "I was almost just another body in the morgue. So please, listen to me."[10]

Young children need to take a trusted adult along when they journey into the vast territory of cyberspace. Just as you wouldn't let your young children wander alone in an unfamiliar neighborhood or send your child into a strange city all by himself, don't leave your child online without guidance. Even older children and teens need rules and limits for the use of the Internet as they explore alone. Protect your children in cyberspace by being aware of their online activities, setting reasonable rules and limits for Internet access, and educating them about the possible hazards of Internet use.

CYBER SAFETY TIPS FOR PARENTS

• Make sure children and teenagers understand the dangers of online use before they have the privilege of using a computer with Internet access.

• Learn about computers so that you can supervise your child's/teen's use. In the same way that you monitor your child's decision to attend a movie or select a video/DVD, it's important to monitor her computer use. Talk to your child/teen often about her online life. Ask your child to show you her favorite sites. Spend time online with your child so that you can learn about her interests and activities. Your kids' superior knowledge of the Internet gives you a wonderful opportunity to invite them to be the experts and teach you something new. New sites and applications become available all the time, so regularly check in with your children about these new developments. Shower them with admiration and respect for their technology skills. You'll be boosting their self-esteem and keeping the doors of communication open.

• Monitor your phone bills and credit card bills for online charges. Many pornographic online vendors charge an access fee to their sites.

• Do not buy your child/teen an external Webcam.

• Keep the computer (with Internet access) in a public area of the house, rather than out of sight in your child's bedroom.

• Set up an agreement and guidelines with your child about the use of the computer. Establish rules for how long he or she can use the computer, and what Web sites the child can and cannot visit.

• Understand the services that your child uses online. Know the Web sites and chat rooms your child visits. As often as you can, accompany teens while they surf the Internet.

• Become acquainted with your child's online friends the same way you get to know your child's neighborhood or school friends.

• Discuss with your child the dangers of meeting a new Internet friend offline. Set a firm rule that the child must get your permission before ever getting together with someone he or she first met online. Only allow such a meeting to occur if a parent accompanies the child and if the meeting is in a public location. Share with your children the stories of teenagers Kristen and Alicia, described above.

• Use parental control and monitoring software as a precaution against accessing adult-oriented Web sites (for example, Net Nanny, Cyber Patrol Parental Controls, KidZui, SpectorPro, and Online Family.Norton). Filtration software, however, should not be relied upon as the sole method of protecting your children. Technology should supplement, not replace, the education you provide about Internet safety.

• Discuss the potential dangers of your children giving out private identity information when chatting online with people they do not know in person. Private identity information includes names (yours and theirs), telephone numbers, addresses, and the name and location of their school. Practice with your children how to respond when someone in a chat room asks for private identity information ("Don't give it, and log off"). Recent research shows that although many youths post personal information online, like on MySpace, posting private identity information by itself does not significantly increase the chances of online victimization. Vulnerability increases when youths give out private information and also engage in "sex talk" in chat rooms.[11]

• If your child gets a suggestive or obscene message, make a copy of the message and report it. GetNetWise.org can help you report online trouble. You can also contact the Cyber Tipline by calling the toll-free number provided by the National Center for Missing and Exploited Children (NCMEC) at (800) 843-5678. You can also report online solicitation on NCMEC's Web site at www.cybertipline.com. It's also a good idea to notify your Internet service provider of the suspicious activity.

• If your child violates the rules and conditions you set for using the Internet, remove his or her privilege of Internet access, and, if possible, prohibit him or her from accessing the Internet at friends' homes, libraries, or schools.

OFF LIMITS SAFETY TIP #27:

Set cyber-safety rules for children and teens.

Rules Parents Can Teach Children for Surfing Safely

- Keep your identity private in chat rooms.
- Do not make sexual statements or engage in sexual conversations while online, especially in chat rooms when you do not know who might be "eavesdropping" on your conversations. No one has the right to talk to you about sexual stuff online.
- Never post your photos on the Internet or send them via e-mail to anyone without your parent's permission.
- Know that not everyone in the chat room is your age or is even there for the same reason you are. Some adults like to trick kids. People you think you "know" on the Internet you really do not know at all. Developing a relationship with an adult you meet online is both illegal and potentially harmful. Remember, every person you meet on the Internet is a stranger.
- Never get together with someone you meet online, unless you have talked to me and gotten my permission first. If you do decide to meet a cyber pal, be sure that it is in a public place and that you bring me or a trusted adult along. Never give the person our home telephone number until after you and I have met the person and we know that the online friend is legitimate and safe.
- Never give out a credit card number online without my permission.
- Do not use a screen name that might be sexually suggestive or that tells either your age or gender.
- If you get any messages that make you feel scared or uncomfortable, do not respond to them. Save copies of any online conversations in which you are bullied, seduced, or harassed. If you are being treated inappropriately, disconnect from the chat, and tell me or a trusted adult immediately, no matter what has occurred. It is never your fault if you get an inappropriate message like that.

"I loved your E-mail, but I thought you'd be older.'"

WARNING SIGNS THAT MAY INDICATE A TEEN IS BEING GROOMED BY AN ONLINE ABUSER

Here are some possible warning signs indicating that your teen may be misusing the Internet or being groomed by an online predator.

- Your teen spends large amounts of time online, especially at night.
- Your teen becomes secretive about his or her time online.
- You find pornography on your home computer.

- Your teen receives phone calls from adults you don't know or is making calls, sometimes long distance, to numbers you don't recognize.
- Your phone bills (for home phones and cell phones) are unusually high and contain many unfamiliar long-distance calls.
- Your teen receives mail, gifts, or packages from someone you don't know.
- Your teen turns the computer monitor off or quickly changes the screen on the monitor when you come into the room.

By taking an active role in your children's and teens' Internet activities, you'll be ensuring that they can benefit from the wealth of valuable information the Internet has to offer, without being exposed to its potential dangers.

In the next and final chapter, we will guide you in helping a sexually abused child, should the need ever arise.

Chapter 9

HOW TO HELP SEXUALLY ABUSED (AND ABUSING) YOUTH

We wrote this book because we firmly believe that parents and other caring adults play very important roles in preventing the sexual abuse of children. The sad reality is that you can implement all of the recommendations in this book, and a child can still be sexually abused. If that should happen, remember, it's not the parent's fault, nor is it the child's fault. The offender is the only person responsible. When children are sexually abused, our responsibilities to them do not end. Sexual abuse is a burden a child should not have to carry alone. There are many ways we can help ease that burden for a child.

In this final chapter, we describe signs of abuse to help you identify and intervene on behalf of a child who is being sexually abused. We suggest how you might respond to a child's disclosure in ways that foster healing rather than continued hurt. We also describe how you can help youths who are exhibiting sexually inappropriate and abusive behaviors. Finally, this chapter guides you through the steps of reporting any known or suspected abuse and explains how to locate mental health services for youthful victims and abusers.

RECOGNIZING SEXUALLY ABUSED CHILDREN: WHAT ARE THE SIGNS?

No one particular sign or symptom indicates a child has been sexually abused. As mentioned in the introduction, about 40 percent of children do not exhibit clinical signs or symptoms. The absence of symptoms does not make the sexual experience acceptable, and asymptomatic children can still benefit from intervention just as children who do show signs can. Of all the signs, problematic or advanced sexual behavior is probably the best indicator that a child is being (or has been) sexually abused, given that repeated genital stimulation can lead to intense and overwhelming states of sexual arousal. In addition to such sexual behaviors, if a child shows signs in more than one way (physical, emotional, or behavioral), displays a drastic change in behavior, or displays such behavior over a prolonged period of time, then such changes are a cause for concern. If you see these behaviors in your child, make an appointment as soon as possible with your child's pediatrician or with a mental health professional who specializes in sexual abuse assessment. Later in the chapter, we suggest how you can locate qualified treatment providers.

OFF LIMITS SAFETY TIP #28:

Know the warning signs of abuse.

Although it is important to know the warning signs of abuse, as we said above, some children do not show obvious signs that abuse is occurring. Do not rule out sexual abuse just because the child is not showing any of the signs that appear on the following lists. What are the warning signs specific to sexual abuse? The signs vary by age.[1]

Infants and toddlers—birth to two years. Preverbal children obviously cannot use words to disclose abuse, but they will demonstrate trauma through physical and emotional signs. Physical signs might include urinary infections, discharges from the penis or vagina, injuries to the genitals or mouth, vomiting, and failure to thrive. Emotional signs might include excessive crying, refusal to eat, inability to be soothed, or extreme fear and anxiety. Sometimes anxiety is displayed in a startle response, which is a physical reaction to a loud noise or sudden movement that causes stiffening of the legs and extension of the arms.

Preschool-age children—three to five years.

Emotional and Behavioral Signs

- Depression and anxiety (being withdrawn, irritable, listless, or clingy, or having separation anxiety or a startle response)

• Excessive fear or refusal to be with a particular person or to go to a particular place

• Sleep disturbances (nightmares, fear of dark, difficulty going to sleep)

• Appetite changes (that are sudden or significant)

• Regression of developmental milestones (an older child acting like a much younger one through such behaviors as bed wetting, thumb sucking, or baby talk)

• Anger or hostility (tantrums, aggressive or abusive behavior toward other children or animals)

• Sudden changes in behavior (cooperative child becomes defiant; happy, outgoing child becomes sad or withdrawn)

Physical Signs

• Frequent complaints about body (stomachaches, vomiting, headaches)

• Pain while urinating or having bowel movements, or frequent urinary tract infections

• Scratches, bruises, rashes, cuts, burns, or other injuries to the genital area

• Difficulty walking or sitting

• Blood or discharge in bedding or underwear (child may hide underwear)

• Sexually transmitted diseases (for example, gonorrhea, syphilis, chlamydia, herpes, or genital warts caused by the human papilloma virus, HPV)

Sexual Behavior Signs

• Advanced knowledge about sex

• Preoccupation with sexual behavior (unable to be redirected)

• Drawings, games, or fantasies that involve inappropriate sexual activities or depict advanced sexual knowledge

- Inappropriate and excessive masturbation (for example, in public places or when the child cannot be redirected; masturbation with objects; rubbing against furniture)
- Frequent exposure of genitals or attempts to expose others' genitals
- Seductive, precocious (advanced) sexual behavior (for example, French kissing)
- Requests for sexual stimulation (for example, child asks to be touched in the genital area)
- Acts out intercourse with peers, toys, or dolls
- Sexual contact with animals (for example, inserts objects into dog's anus)
- Inserts objects into own vagina and/or anus

School-age children—six to twelve years. Children in this age group are more likely to show problems at school, such as learning difficulties, declining grades, difficulties with concentration and attention, and poor peer relations. In contrast, other abused children appear to be perfect students and are overly compliant with authority figures. Acting-out behaviors such as delinquency, stealing, lying, keeping secrets, running away, and substance abuse might also be seen among such youths in this age group.

These youths may also show emotional problems such as depression, guilt, anxiety, hostility, aggression, suicide attempts, tics, phobias, or obsessions. The physical signs in school-age children are similar to those seen among preschool children. Other red flags include talking about an older "special friend," or having new clothes, toys, or money (not given to them by their parents).

Preteens and adolescents—12 and older. The behavioral, emotional, and physical indicators that preteen and adolescent children exhibit are similar to those of school-age children.

- Statements that their bodies are ruined, damaged, or dirtied, or that something is wrong with their genitals
- Statements indicating depression and low self-esteem ("I wish I were dead")

- Running away from home or refusal to attend school
- Self-mutilation (cutting or burning one's body, hair pulling)
- Drug or alcohol use
- Fire setting
- Spending excessive time with a "special adult friend" or maintaining secret Internet friends
- Withdrawal from family and/or friends
- Mistrust or reluctance to get physically or emotionally close to others
- Suicidal threats or attempts
- Eating disorders (the child overeats or undereats, resulting in a marked change in body weight)
- Unusual level of modesty or body shame (for example, extreme reluctance to change clothes or shower around others, like in gym class)

Sexual Behaviors in Preteens and Adolescents

- Having sexual intercourse at an early age or with older partners
- Becoming pregnant
- Having many sexual partners (sexually promiscuous)
- Exchanging sex for money
- Excessive masturbation
- Addiction to pornography
- Deviant sexual behaviors (for example, voyeurism and exhibitionism)
- Forced touching of younger children's genitals
- Fear of sexual intimacy

RESPONDING TO CHILDREN'S DISCLOSURES

When children seek help in situations as serious and confusing as sexual abuse, their approach is usually indirect rather than direct with their disclosures. Do you think a child would ever say, "Hey Mom, Dad, I have something to tell you. I was sexually abused at school today and I need your help." That's not how children disclose. Instead, kids are much more likely to make indirect statements ("I don't like that person") or they may reveal information through their behavior. In her book, *Miss America By Day*, Marilyn Van Derbur reports that her sister was being raped by their father in her bedroom at night. Her sister tried to tell her mother when she asked for a lock on her bedroom door.[2] Like this girl, most children test adults to see if they will be listened to, believed, and helped. It is important for parents and other caring adults to actively listen to children's statements, questions, and behaviors. Pay attention if a child makes negative comments about a person ("He's mean") or if a child doesn't want to be with a particular person, especially if it's an abrupt turnaround. If a child suddenly refuses to go to a friend's or relative's home for no apparent reason, find out why. Here, an adult survivor of sibling abuse describes how she "tried" to tell through her behavior:

> *Between the ages of 8 and 12, I was raped by my stepbrother, who was two years older than me. Our parents were divorced, and every other weekend, I and my two brothers would all spend the weekend at my father's house. There was only one bedroom available for all us kids, so we took turns sleeping in the bedroom and the living room. One weekend I would get the bedroom and my brothers would sleep in the living room; the next weekend the boys would sleep in the bedroom and I would sleep on the couch. When I slept in the bedroom, I was safe, because I could lock the door. The weekends I slept in the living room, my stepbrother would come out of the bedroom during the night and abuse me. Every weekend it was my turn to sleep in the living room, I would cry uncontrollably and beg to sleep in the bedroom. I was scolded and called "spoiled" and "selfish" and told that I needed to learn to share.*

OFF LIMITS SAFETY TIP #29:

Help children tell about sexual abuse.

In order for children to tell parents or other caring adults about a concern as serious as sexual abuse, we must make it safe for them to tell. In order for children to tell a trusted adult about an abusive situation, they need to be assured of the following:

- Children must be told and must truly believe that telling about any inappropriate touching is the right thing to do. They need both the permission and the language to tell. They must know that even if they feel embarrassed, guilty, dirty, bad, or ashamed, they should still tell. Even if they've kept it a secret for a long time, they must be reassured that it's never too late to tell. And most importantly, they must know that no matter what the circumstances, abuse is never the child's fault. The abuser is always responsible for what has happened.

- Children must know that you will believe them when they share their worries with you, and that you will take their concerns seriously. There are people who believe that children fabricate stories about being sexually abused. Actually, it is extremely rare (only 2 percent of cases)[3] for children to lie about sexual abuse, saying it has happened to them when it has not. Young children do not have the sexual knowledge to make up stories of abuse. A young child who says, "His penis spit up milk" cannot fabricate these details without actually witnessing ejaculation. Older children and teenagers might have more sexual knowledge and experience, but they, too, almost never allege abuse if it has not happened. Those rare situations in which children have lied about abuse have been in divorce or custody cases when the child has been coached by a parent to accuse the other parent. In these cases, the adults, not the children, are lying. Although it is rare for children and teens to fabricate sexual abuse when it has not happened, it is more common for older children and especially teenagers to lie by denying that abuse has occurred, when it actually has.

- Children must believe that you are strong enough to handle anything they tell you. They need to know that you will not be destroyed or crumble because of anything they disclose. They must know that you are their foundation, and that they can come to you for support. Most importantly, children must know that you will put their needs first and that you will take care of them.

• Children must know that they will not be punished for being honest and for telling you the truth, even if they have broken a rule. Let's say a child tells you that she stole something from the store. If you punish her for stealing when she admitted to a wrongdoing, what will she learn from the punishment? Most likely that it's better not to confess. Instead, you might praise her for telling you the truth, and then you could ask her how the store owner might feel about having something stolen from the store, or how she might feel if someone stole something from her. You could also have her take the item back to the store and apologize to the owner—turning this negative situation into a valuable teachable moment. The most important response, however, would be to praise her for telling you the truth. By praising children for admitting when they have made a mistake or broken a rule, you are increasing the likelihood that they will feel safe talking with you about their life experiences, both positive and negative ones. Use the same principle if your child is ever touched inappropriately, especially if the touching occurs when he or she has not followed your rules. Children must know that even if they have broken a rule, you still love them, and that you will put their safety first.

Here's what happened when a child feared being punished for breaking rules:

Anna and her best friend Tala are both nine years old. The two girls regularly play together in the neighborhood. Anna's mother set down a rule that Anna could never go into the neighbor's house across the street. Pointing to the neighbor's house, her mother repeated this rule often, saying, "Do not go in that guy's house, or I'll kill you." (Of course she did not mean she would literally kill Anna, but she was emphasizing the seriousness of the rule.) This particular neighbor was quite persuasive, however, and he finally lured the two girls into his home with offers of soda and cookies. While there, Anna was forced to sit on the man's lap and French-kiss him. Then the neighbor raped her friend Tala. When Anna was asked if she had told her mother what happened, she replied, "No. She said she would kill me if I went into his house."

• Children must know that they will not be blamed for abuse. One survivor told us about the time she was about 12 and her mother's boyfriend put his hands up her shirt to "check on whether her breasts were developing normally." When she told her mother, her mother replied, "That's because you walk around in those tank tops flirting with him and flaunting your body." She never told her mother about any more of his touches. If children feel responsible for their abuse or if they worry about being blamed, then it is unlikely that they will disclose. In contrast, if they believe they will be taken seriously and listened to, there is a better chance that they will tell. Children need to be reassured that it is never their fault if somebody jeopardizes their safety. Under no circumstances is it ever a child's fault or responsibility when he or she is sexually abused. Children cannot consent to sexual activities.

• A child must know that even if someone tells her to keep sexual touching a secret, she should still tell. Let her know she should tell you or another trusted adult, even if the person requesting the silence is someone she loves. Talk with her about the tricks or threats someone may use to get her not to tell, like "I'll hurt your Mommy if you tell." Let the child know that you will protect her from harm and that her safety is more important than anything else. Sometimes a child fears the consequences of telling about abuse (the offender going to jail or her family splitting apart). Stress how important it is for the child to tell a safe adult, so that that person can help stop the abuse.

She needs to know that her personal safety is far more important than whether or not the family stays together or the abuser goes to jail. This point will be an emotional and potentially frightening one for the child, and will need great care and attentiveness on the adult's part.

• Finally, every child must have a hero. All children need caring adults in their lives who can recognize the signs of sexual abuse and can intervene. All children need someone who will listen to them and believe them. An abused child needs someone who is brave enough to believe her and powerful enough to stop the abuser. Counter the abuser's power with your own. Be a child's hero!

OFF LIMITS SAFETY TIP #30:

Know how to respond to a child's disclosure.

Helpful healing responses:

- Remain calm in the child's presence. Focus on the child's needs. No matter how upset, angry, or afraid you are, try to control your emotions and stay focused on what the child needs.
- Believe the child and reassure the child that it's not his or her fault. "I believe what you are telling me, and I want you to know that this is not your fault. You didn't do anything wrong."
- Express sympathy. "I am so sorry this happened to you."
- Affirm the child's courage to tell. "I am so proud of you for telling me. You are so brave." "That took a lot of courage to tell me." "You did the right thing by telling me."
- Acknowledge and accept the child's feelings. "It's OK to be scared/sad/mad/worried."
- Support the child. "I am here to keep you safe." "I love you and will always love you, no matter what."
- Tell the child what you will do. "We are going to go to the doctor" or "We are going to talk to some special people at Social Services who help kids stay safe" or "We know it may not be easy to talk about, but there are other people who need to know what happened so that they can help [the abuser] stop doing this to other children." Offer protection to the child, and also let the child know that you will take steps to stop the abuse.
- Seek medical assistance for the child, if necessary, and psychological support for the child and family.

If the sexual activity has caused injury to the child's body, a medical examination is important. A sensitive physician can offer children support and reassurance that their bodies will heal. Medical professionals can provide treatment for any injuries or diseases resulting from the abuse. And physical evidence needs to be collected in the event that the case goes to court.

In addition to medical support, psychological counseling is absolutely critical. Giving the child a safe and supportive relationship with someone who is skilled in working with sexually abused children can help the healing process and minimize long-term trauma of sexual abuse. Oftentimes, all family members can benefit from counseling where they can discuss what happened and how it has affected them. With the help of qualified professionals, the abuse can be put in proper perspective. Therapy can be beneficial for many reasons, but unfortunately few victims of sexual abuse get professional help. Some of the many reasons victims never receive counseling or therapy include:

- parents' fears about making the child "relive" the abuse again
- parents' belief that outside help is unnecessary, preferring instead to handle it within the family
- family's limited financial resources or lack of health insurance
- a community's lack of qualified therapists
- parents' beliefs that the child is "adjusting to it," is "resilient," or will "forget about it"
- parents' mistrust of authorities
- parents' concerns that other people will find out about it and bring shame to the family (for example, some parents may worry that cooperating with authorities will make it more likely that word will get out that their daughter has been "ruined" and spoiled for marriage; in some cultures, the entire family is considered tainted if one of the daughters has been sexually victimized)[4]

Unhelpful, re-traumatizing responses:

- Expressing self-blame to your child. "How could I have let this happen to you?" When adults blame themselves—they shouldn't have chosen the babysitter, left the child alone, etc.—the child may feel responsible for adults blaming themselves. Children can also misinterpret the parent's anger about the abuse and think that their parents are angry at them. Children also want to protect their parents from feeling hurt and may do so by recanting, changing the story, or shutting down altogether. If your child has been a victim of sexual abuse, it is important that you discuss any feelings of anger or guilt with another adult, rather than expressing negative feelings to your child. Ask friends, loved ones, or professionals for support. It is a parent's job to take care of the child's feelings, not the other way around.

• Blaming the child for the abuse. "Why didn't you say 'No'?" "Why didn't you yell or run?" "This is what you get for dressing the way you do." "How could you let this happen?" "You must've asked for it." Under no circumstances is abuse ever a child's fault. The responsibility always lies with the offender, whether the abuser is an older child, a teenager, or an adult. Children are not able to consent to sexual activities—they lack the ability to understand the consequences involved and are unable to freely say "No." When children are blamed for sexual abuse, they are victimized twice—first by the abuser, and second by the person blaming them.

• Crying, yelling, or expressing anger in the child's presence. "I'll kill him."

• Overprotecting the child. "You are never leaving my sight again."

• Emphasizing or labeling the child as a victim or as "permanently damaged goods." "You poor thing."

• Promising to keep the disclosure a secret, when you really intend to report. Promising to keep the disclosure a secret can lead to broken promises and a further betrayal of a child's trust in adults.

• Investigating the allegation, especially by asking leading questions about details (for example, "Did he touch your privates?"). Asking about details can change a child's memory for the event. Any questions you ask should be only open-ended ones ("What happened next?"). Let the authorities investigate.

• Confronting the offender. Leave that job to the authorities.

Here's what happened when Lori's offender was confronted:

> *Lori told her schoolteacher that her father was sneaking in her bed at night and touching her under her T-shirt and underwear. Instead of reporting it directly to social services, the teacher reported it to the principal, who mistakenly called Lori's mother. When Lori arrived home, her mother was angry with her for telling her teacher about "family business." Lori's father threatened to leave the family if she told anybody else. The next day Lori told her teacher she made up the whole story.*

- Denying or questioning whether the abuse occurred. "This couldn't have happened. You must be dreaming." "Don't make up stories like that." "Are you sure?" "Why don't we all just forget it happened?"

Here's an example of the effect that denial can have on a child:

> *In her book,* After All, *actress Mary Tyler Moore wrote about her parents' best friend, Mr. Archer, fondling her when she was six. When she told her mother about what Mr. Archer had done to her, her mother said, "No. That's not true." Ms. Moore remembers that her mother said three words that changed her life forever— "It didn't happen." Mary continued, "I never felt the same about my mother after that. Her denial had abused me far more than her friend."*[5]

Appropriate responses to children's disclosures will help children heal from the trauma of sexual abuse. Not only can parents and other caring adults recognize and respond to children who may be experiencing abuse, but those adults can also help youth who may be reenacting their own sexual trauma through inappropriate sexual behaviors with other children.

RECOGNIZING SEXUALLY ABUSIVE BEHAVIORS

Parents and other concerned adults need to know the differences between normal sexual curiosity and sexually abusive behaviors. What are those differences? Normal sexual play is consensual; there is no emotional or physical coercion involved. In contrast, sexually abusive youths may have sexual interactions with other children that involve dominance, coercion, threats, force, aggression, and compulsivity. Children who display sexually abusive behaviors often continue the behavior, even after an adult asks them to stop. Here are some other warning signs of problematic sexual play:

- Age: One child/teen is more than three or four years older than the other child (state laws vary)
- Size: One child/teen is much larger than the other
- Status: One child/teen has more power, advanced knowledge, or greater status than the other
- Type of play: Sexual play is frequent and intense and may have a compulsive quality
- Harm: Sexual behavior causes significant emotional distress or physical injury to the other child
- Coercion: Child/teen uses physical and/or emotional coercion to gain compliance or reduce the resistance of another child (for example, the abuser uses bribes or threats or restrains the child)[6]
- Secrecy: Child/teen convinces (through intimidations or threats) the younger child to keep the activity a secret
- Advanced sex: Sexual behaviors are of an advanced or sophisticated nature (for example, mimicking oral sex or intercourse, or when any type of penetration occurs, whether with a finger, object, or penis)

Here are other signs and behaviors typical of youths who may be sexually acting out with children:

- Has sexual fantasies involving children (having sexual dreams about younger children; verbalizing the desire to have sex with a young child)
- Practices voyeurism ("peeping tom": spying in the windows of girls' homes or sneaking into the girls' locker room to peep at the girls undressing)
- Practices exhibitionism (exposing genitals to younger children)
- Engages in sexually explicit conversations with younger children (a teenage babysitter who talks about sexual acts with young children)
- Insists on hugging, touching, kissing, tickling, wrestling with, or holding a child even when the child does not want this affection

- Shows sexual material (like pornography) to younger children
- Encourages silence or secrets in the child
- Often has a "special" child friend, and maybe a different one from year to year
- Is overly interested in the sexuality or maturity of children (such as a teen who constantly talks about the developing body of a younger child)
- Plays younger-aged games with children (for example, plays house, dolls, or doctor)
- Spends a large amount of spare time with younger children, and does not have similarly aged friends
- Spends a lot of time looking at pornographic Web sites
- Fondles younger children's genitals

DISTINGUISHING BETWEEN NORMAL AND PROBLEMATIC SEXUAL BEHAVIORS

We invite you to apply your knowledge about normal sexual development (from chapter 6) and what you have learned about problematic sexual behaviors to the following scenarios. For each of the following situations, ask yourself, is the behavior normal or problematic?

1. Your five-year-old daughter has her five-year-old playmate over. You are making them lunch and you hear giggling coming from the bathroom. You go to check on the two girls and find that they have their pants and underwear off and are taking turns standing over the toilet pretending to pee like boys.

2. Your four-year-old son and his four-year-old male playmate are spending the afternoon together. They are playing with action figures in his room and you are studying in your office across the hall. You hear them whispering and laughing and you peek into the room. They both have their clothes off and are sitting across from each other talking about their penises.

3. Your seven-year-old daughter has her seven-year-old girlfriend over to spend the night. An hour after you put them in their bunk beds, you go to check on them. You find both girls in one bunk, naked, with their mouths on each other's genitals. They jump up when they see you and one of the girls begins to cry.

4. Your four-year-old son comes home from preschool and tells you that a four-year-old girl in his preschool class got on his mat at nap time and said, "Let me touch your pee-pee, or I won't be your friend ever again."

5. Your eight-year-old daughter and her same-age friend are changing their clothes to get ready for their dance class. They are taking longer than usual, so you go into your daughter's room to nudge them along. Both girls are naked, sitting in front of the mirror, looking at their own and each other's vulvas. They quickly drape their clothes over themselves and look embarrassed.

6. Your five-year-old daughter tells you that while changing into her swimsuit at camp today, her six-year-old friend stuck his finger into her vagina. She tells you that it hurt and scared her.

7. You're driving in the car with your four-year-old daughter playing "What if" games and discussing body-safety rules. Your daughter starts to cry and tells you that at the family holiday party last week, her five-year-old cousin shoved her in the closet and stuck his tongue in her mouth and threatened her not to tell.

8. Your 12-year-old daughter babysits for your eight-year-old son. One day after she took care of him, your son starts asking you questions about sex and tells you that his sister is "teaching him sex." He tells you that, "She put her finger in my butt and it hurt."

9. Your six-year-old daughter and her six-year-old friend are playing house and pretending to get married. Their play involves kissing and hugging.

10. A nine-year-old girl was observed at school rubbing the crotch of a five-year-old boy on the playground.

Normal sexual behaviors (examples 1, 2, 5, and 9) are lighthearted, exploratory, and consensual, whereas problematic sexual behaviors (examples 3, 4, 6, 7, 8, and 10) involve coercion, secrecy, advanced sexual behaviors, and sometimes threats. It's as important for adults to respond supportively to children's "normal" sexual behaviors as it is for them to respond to problematic sexual behaviors.

RESPONDING TO SEXUALLY OFFENDING YOUTH

Let's look at how a parent might respond to problematic sexual behavior in a teenager:

Antonia received a call from her neighbors, who had discovered that Antonia's 14-year-old son Marcus was being sexual with their seven-year-old son. Although the neighboring mother preferred to deal with the problem privately, the father had called the police. The neighbor mother said, "Antonia, this is very difficult for me to tell you, but I need to out of concern for the safety of both of our children. Marcus has been playing a touching game with Tomás, where they rubbed each other's penises. He told Tomás not to tell anyone or they'd both get in trouble."

Antonia experienced a flood of emotions. She had a brief moment of denial when she thought the neighbors must be mistaken; her child would never molest anyone. Surely the boys were just playing an innocent game with each other. When the neighbor gave her more details about what had occurred (that it involved repetitive mutual touching of genitals, secrecy, and threats), Antonia's denial gave way, and she was flooded with fear, shame, embarrassment, and guilt.

Imagine for a moment that your teenager was sexually abusing a younger child. How would you feel? What actions might these feelings lead you to take? Parents have told us that they often minimize the behavior (for example, "Boys will be boys"), believe the child will grow out of it, or attempt to deal with it privately and not seek professional help. Like Antonia, most parents want to protect their child from the shame of public exposure or legal consequences, even when their child was the one initiating the abuse.

When adults ignore or minimize sexual misconduct in children or teenagers, however, these youths never have an opportunity to learn that it is morally and legally wrong to coerce other children into sexual activities. If adults react negatively to these behaviors and convey a strong message that sex with children is wrong, then there is a better chance they can stop the sexual misconduct and thus prevent other children from being victimized. Early discovery and treatment of sexually offending youth is essential if childhood sexual abuse is ever going to be eliminated. In a letter to the editor of the *PARENTalk Newsletter* (produced by Stop It Now!), a mother described what it was like being the parent of both a child who had been offending and a child who had been victimized. Her older son Troy, 15, was sexually abusing her younger son Ted, 12. She described how confused she was feeling, as well as guilty. She felt ashamed that she cared for and wanted to protect Troy even though he had hurt Ted. She offered this advice to other parents with a child who has sexual behavior problems: "Your child is still young and resilient; it is never too late for change. Seize the chance now—get help for your child so that the behaviors do not progress into adolescence and adulthood."

OFF LIMITS SAFETY TIP #31:

Know how to respond to youths with sexual behavior problems.

How do you respond if you suspect or learn that a child is exhibiting sexual behavior problems? First, talk with the child. Let him or her know that you care about and love him or her and that you want to help. Label the behavior with words and describe your concern or feelings. For example, you can say, "I see that you are looking at pictures of naked children and that concerns me."[7] Use active listening skills. Listen closely to what the youth says and watch how he or she responds. The youth might minimize or deny the behavior, change the story, blame the other child, or even admit to the behavior. Here's Antonia's conversation with her son Marcus:

> *Antonia: "I need to talk to you about what happened at Tomás's house. But let me start out by saying that no matter what has happened, I will always love you. Tomás's mom told me that Tomás said you made him rub your penis, and that he'd be in big trouble if he told anyone."*
> *Marcus: "What? We were just messing around."*
> *Antonia: "Can you tell me what you mean by 'messing around'? I know this may be scary to talk about, but we have to. Remember, I love you and want to help you."*
> *Marcus: "You know, Mom, Tomás lies a lot. He asked me to rub his penis."*
> *Antonia: "I'm very concerned about this situation. We need to talk about it with a counselor who helps kids with their problems."*

Even if your child denies or minimizes the problem, contact a therapist who works with youths with sexual behavior problems. You can find qualified therapists by contacting your local mental health center or your state's mental health licensing board. Each state maintains a listing of psychiatrists, psychologists, social workers, and counselors available in your city or town. Here are three organizations that can assist with referrals:

- Association for the Treatment of Sexual Abusers (ATSA, at www.atsa.com)
- Child Molestation Research and Prevention Institute (www.cmrpi.org)
- Safer Society Foundation (www.safersociety.org)

Once you've made contact, ask if the organization specializes in assessing and treating youths with sexual behavior problems. For example, Antonia might say, "I just learned that my teenage son has been making a young boy touch his penis. I'm frightened and worried, and my son needs help. Do you treat teenagers with these kinds of problems or know where I can get help?" Asking for help would take a lot of courage for any parent, but it is definitely the right thing to do.

Keep the lines of communication open, and support your child during counseling. Review body-safety rules and set clear boundaries regarding privacy and touching. Eliminate all unsupervised contact with younger children until the assessment is completed.

Finally, be sure to seek support for yourself. Reach out to loved ones or professionals for emotional assistance during this troubling time.

REPORTING CHILD SEXUAL ABUSE

Certain groups of people are required by law to report suspected sexual abuse of children. These groups are called "mandated reporters." Although each state has different groups identified in the list of reporters, most states include teachers, day-care workers, mental health professionals, law enforcement personnel, clergy, and medical professionals (doctors, nurses, dentists). If a mandated reporter knows or suspects that a child is either a victim or perpetrator of sexual abuse, she or he must notify the authorities (see Safety Tip #32 for details). It is not the responsibility of a mandated reporter to acquire details about the abuse. The person only has to report known or suspected abuse. If a mandated reporter does not notify the authorities within a specific time frame, he or she can be held personally liable. Mandated reporters are not liable for unfounded reports; they are required to report abuse only when a child has disclosed abuse or when a suspicion of abuse exists. Mandated reporters are not permitted to notify parents before contacting the authorities. Any adult can report a suspicion of abuse. When a citizen reports abuse, he or she can do so anonymously.

Reporting child sexual abuse is essential for both the victim and the abuser, but sometimes adults are reluctant to report, oftentimes for these reasons:

- They have heard stories about social service agencies taking children away from their parents.
- They fear retaliation from the alleged abuser.
- They do not want to re-traumatize their child.
- They do not want their child to go through the legal system.
- They do not want to get the abuser in trouble, especially if they care about him or her.
- They want to handle the matter privately.
- They're not 100 percent sure it's abuse.

Although all of these fears and concerns are understandable, when adults do not report suspected or known sexual abuse of children, it leaves other children at risk. If a report is not made, authorities cannot stop the perpetrator from sexually abusing other children in the community. Adults have the responsibility and the power to break the silence and to protect children.

In their parent's guide to healing and recovery titled *When Your Child Has Been Molested*, authors Hagans and Case describe one mother's response to learning of her daughter's abuse:

> *The pain of what I experienced was almost indescribable. When I first heard that my husband had sexually molested our little girl, I was devastated. I went to my minister, who said that in order for the family to be healed, I must report the abuse. I became very angry. I had wanted my minister "to make it all go away." I thought that if my husband became religious, the responsibility for the abuse and for the family's healing would be put on someone else's shoulders. My minister said that part of the*

healing process was to bring the incest out into the open. He guided me to a therapist who knew how to work with sexual abuse within families. I eventually realized, with the help of both my minister and therapist, that I had done the right thing for my child, myself, and my husband by reporting the abuse.[8]

OFF LIMITS SAFETY TIP #32:

Know how to report suspected sexual abuse.

Two agencies are designated to handle reports of childhood sexual abuse: Child Protective Services and law enforcement. If the abuser lives in the home (for example, a sibling, parent, blood relative, or anyone in a position of trust over the child), then contact your local department of social/human services or your state Child Protective Service agency. If the person does not live in the home, contact your local police department, county sheriff's department, or district attorney's office. Social service agencies and law enforcement departments work together on sexual abuse cases, so either agency can help. If you feel uncertain about whom to contact, call the national organization Child Help USA, whose hotline can offer you guidance (1-800-4AChild or 1-800-422-4453). When suspected abuse is reported to Child Protective Services, the reporting person will be asked to provide the child's name, date of birth, parent's name, details of the suspected abuse, the name and address of the alleged offender and his or her relationship to the child, and the location where the abuse occurred. You do not have to be 100 percent sure it's abuse. Sexual abuse only needs to be suspected to be reported. The investigating agency is responsible for determining whether criminal behavior has occurred. People who report sexual abuse in good faith are protected from civil and criminal court action.

Our wish is that all children grow up free from sexual abuse. But the reality is that as long as abusers exist, children will be sexually victimized. We hope this chapter has prepared you to help abused youth by identifying them and helping them to heal. Children who receive counseling for sexual abuse are much less likely to abuse other children or to carry the trauma into their own adulthood. When sexually acting-out youth receive counseling, they, too, have a better chance of becoming sexually healthy adults. Your courage in helping children who have suffered from abuse can give them the courage to heal.

Epilogue

REVISITING OUR SURVIVORS

We now invite you to apply the knowledge you have learned from *Off Limits* to the situations surrounding Sasha, Gustavo, Laura, and Monique. Using this information, consider how their abuse could have been prevented in the first place, or how intervention early in the abuse process could have minimized the harm.

THE ROLE OF PARENTS IN PREVENTING SEXUAL ABUSE

One commonality with the children in our four cases is that not one was educated about body safety. As we suggested in chapter 6, when children are taught body-safety rules within the context of sexuality education, it can reduce their vulnerability to abuse. What if these four children had been taught (either by their parents or by school personnel) that if anyone ever asked them to engage in sexual touching, they could say "No!" and tell their parent or another trusted adult? When parents establish a "no-secrets" rule in their homes and also make sure that their children know they do not have to comply with unsafe or inappropriate requests from authority figures, those parents can reduce their children's vulnerabilities to abuse. What if those four children in chapter 1 had known not to keep secrets about touching and had known that they could refuse to obey an authority figure's unsafe request? What if the children had been told that even if someone touched their private parts, it was never their fault? If Sasha had had this type of education, perhaps she would have been empowered to tell Maria about Mike's sexual touches.

If Mo had learned body-safety rules and knew she would be believed, maybe she would have told someone that Miss Jenkins was sexually abusing her. Had Gustavo been taught the "no-secrets" rule, perhaps he would have refused to keep Kevin's secrets. And perhaps if Laura and her siblings had had frequent discussions with their parents about body safety within the context of healthy sexual development, the sibling abuse could have been prevented.

The parents of Sasha, Gus, Laura, and Mo had a lot in common. They all loved their children and did not intentionally put them in harm's way. But because these parents were uninformed about childhood sexual abuse and abusers, they were unable to prevent an abusive stepfather, sibling, church leader, and teacher/coach from sexually abusing their children. As we said in the introduction, "smarter adults mean safer children." Like thousands of other children, Sasha, Gus, Laura, and Mo were vulnerable to abuse because their parents did not know about abusers' common characteristics and patterns of behaviors, and they did not recognize their children's cries for help.

Maria married a man whom she believed had her daughter's best interests in mind. Maria wanted Sasha to have a loving, involved father and she truly believed Mike fit the bill. Like many people, Maria assumed that a child sexual abuser would have sexual interests only in children. But during their courtship and early years of marriage, Maria and Mike had a very active and enjoyable sexual relationship. Because he was obviously not a pedophile, Maria never thought that Mike would use her daughter to meet his sexual and emotional needs. Also, Maria did not know about situational abusers, nor was she aware that stepfathers are three times more likely to sexually abuse their stepdaughters than biological fathers.[1] What could Maria have done to screen Mike for his potential to abuse her daughter? Maria could have asked about his childhood sexual experiences. Perhaps if she had, Mike would have told her that he had had a close relationship with his teenage female babysitter when he was young—a relationship that included both emotional nurturing and sexual touching. Together they could have talked about how his early sexual experience might affect his ability to parent Sasha. Looking back, we also see that Mike gave some clues (like being possessive of Sasha, limiting her contact with her friends, and encouraging Maria to accept catering jobs so that he and Sasha could go out on "dates"), but Maria did not recognize these actions as signs of an incestuous relationship.

Like Maria, Rosie had done what seemed to be a responsible and loving thing for her child. She had enrolled Gustavo in activities that supported his interests and had given him a chance to socialize with peers in a safe setting—a church. She also had given Gustavo the benefit of the mentoring provided by Kevin, the youth pastor. How could she have prevented Gustavo from being sexually abused? Perhaps she could have met with the church administrator and Kevin and informed them about her off limits safety practices, including that Gustavo had been taught body-safety rules about not touching private parts and not keeping secrets from her. Mo's mother, Wendy, also lacked information about sexual abusers (particularly female abusers) and did not recognize the signs that Miss Jenkins was trying to gain her daughter's sexual compliance. Neither Rosie nor Wendy questioned an authority figure's spending time alone with their children, inviting the children to sleepovers, or giving them expensive gifts. When parents know that these kinds of behaviors might reflect someone's sexual interest in children, they can intervene and prevent abuse.

As we have seen with Laura, sibling incest can sometimes cause serious and long-term psychological trauma. Sibling incest is also of concern because of how common it is in families. Fortunately, sibling incest can be prevented if parents educate all of their children about privacy and inappropriate touching. Like the others, Laura's parents were not informed about childhood sexual abuse, nor did they teach body-safety rules to their children. Discussions about sexuality, appropriate touching, secrets, and in-home privacy were lacking. In fact, Chris violated his sisters' personal privacy on a regular basis. If Laura's parents had recognized violation of privacy as a sign of possible abuse and actively listened to their daughters' complaints about Chris's behavior, then perhaps the abuse could have been prevented. Unfortunately, Chris continued to be left in charge of his sisters while the parents worked late hours. Chris was afforded the access, privacy, and control he needed to abuse Laura. It's quite likely that Laura's abuse could have been prevented if her parents had known about the risk of letting a teenage boy who was already exhibiting problematic behaviors supervise young children. Laura's parents were also uninformed about the potential danger of a teenager's unsupervised Internet access. Chris spent hours surfing the Internet on the computer that was in his bedroom with no protective software installed on it. Chris's parents did not discuss cyber safety with their son. Instead, Chris browsed pornographic Web sites as often as he liked. Several of these sites required credit card access, which appeared on his parents' credit card statements. As discussed in chapter 8, this would have been a perfect opportunity to intervene and possibly stop the development of Chris's sexual behavior problems. Getting Chris help for his problem most likely would have both prevented Laura's abuse and gotten Chris the help he needed to stop his sexually offending behaviors.

CARING ADULTS AS PART OF THE PREVENTION TEAM

Other adults also missed opportunities to intervene and help these four children. Although medical professionals treated Sasha for repeated urinary tract infections, they never performed a pelvic examination or asked questions about possible sexual abuse. Her teachers were aware of her acute level of anxiety, perfectionism, and crying spells, but no one identified these behaviors as warning signs of abuse. What if a teacher had referred her to the school counselor who could have helped Sasha reveal what was going on? Sasha needed a hero, but the adults around her did not recognize and respond to the signs of her abuse. Sasha's eventual heroes turned out to be her friend and the friend's mom, who reported the abuse to social services. Only then did the abuse stop.

If the church administrators had conducted a thorough screening and background check when Kevin applied for the youth pastor position, then Kevin might not have had access to the youth in the preteen program. Even if Kevin had passed the pre-employment screening, all faith-based communities need policies regarding adult-child interactions outside of church-sponsored events. What if the church had required that any employee notify a supervisor of his or her wishes to be in contact with children outside of church activities? Other adults in Gustavo's life could have intervened, as well. For example, the teachers noticed Gustavo's behavioral problems, including his extreme self-hatred, difficult peer relationships, failing grades, and disruptive classroom behavior. A referral to the school counselor was made, but the counselor missed an opportunity to help Gustavo tell about his abuse. Instead, the counselor recommended that he be evaluated for hyperactivity, and the pediatrician prescribed medication for this disorder. Although difficulty concentrating and disruptive behaviors are indeed signs of hyperactivity, they are also signs of sexual abuse. What if the doctor had asked questions to determine if sexual abuse played a role in his difficulties? Unfortunately, the medical professional did not ask Gustavo the kinds of questions that might have helped him to disclose his abuse.

Laura's symptoms of sibling abuse also went unnoticed by adults at her school. Laura went from enjoying school and being an involved student to skipping school and failing her classes. The gynecologist Laura visited to obtain contraceptives also missed a golden opportunity to help Laura disclose her abuse. When health-care providers include questions about sexual abuse in their routine screenings, abused adolescents are more likely to talk about their sexual victimization. Unfortunately, Laura was not asked.

Mo was frequently seen leaving the school parking lot with Miss Jenkins. As described in chapter 7, it is important that schools establish policies about teachers spending time alone with students after school hours. Did any administrator or colleague of Miss Jenkins notice the time she was spending with this student? If so, perhaps a staff member at the school could have questioned her actions. Other school personnel could have intervened when they noticed Mo's grades worsening. Once Mo's "relationship" with Miss Jenkins became sexual, Mo lost all interest in schoolwork and her grades dropped. Her sudden depressed mood and lack of interest in school were very obvious changes. Whenever teachers see these kinds of behavioral changes, it is important that they intervene, perhaps by referring the child in question to a school counselor and by informing parents about the changes they have observed.

CONCLUSION

Throughout this book we have described these and other cases to demonstrate how easy it is for abusers to gain children's sexual compliance and silence.

If you know an adolescent who is sexually promiscuous and is cutting on her body, ask questions and intervene. If you have a student who begins to show extreme signs of perfectionism, ask questions and intervene. You are now informed about how abusers gain children's sexual compliance. If you know of a spiritual leader who is asking children to spend time alone outside of church-related activities, ask questions and intervene. When a teacher is spending an inordinate amount of time alone with a student outside of school, ask questions and intervene.

Off Limits has served its purpose if it has convinced you of the importance of:

- knowing the common characteristics of sexual abusers;
- understanding the process often used by abusers to gain a child's sexual compliance;
- responding and intervening when you have suspicions of abuse;
- making your home off limits;
- empowering children with body-safety knowledge and skills to keep themselves safe;
- raising sexually healthy children who will not sexually offend against others;
- talking about sexual abuse and its prevention with caregivers and authority figures; and
- taking a proactive role in stopping the epidemic of childhood sexual abuse.

It's up to us to be heroes for children and the guardians of their safety. Thank you for being willing to step forward and help all children grow up free from sexual exploitation and abuse.

—

Be the change you wish to see in the world.[2]

—Gandhi

APPENDIXES

APPENDIX 1

OFF LIMITS KIDS, HOMES, AND COMMUNITIES

OFF LIMITS SAFETY TIPS

The following pages, "I Am an Off Limits Kid," "We Have an Off Limits Home," "We Live in an Off Limits Community," and "Off Limits Safety Tips" may be copied by the reader for personal use.

The following pages are also available as pdfs, which may downloaded and printed, at the Safer Society Web site (www.safersociety.org).

I AM AN OFF LIMITS KID!

I know I'm the boss of my body.

•

I know the names of my private parts.

•

I know to take a buddy and tell Mom/Dad where I'm going.

•

I know to ask first before I accept gifts or a ride or help an adult.

•

I know that it's not okay for other kids, teens, or adults to touch children's private parts.

•

I know never to keep secrets about touching private parts.

•

I can choose how to show affection.

•

I know my parents will always believe me.

•

I know it's not okay for adults to show kids pictures or movies of people who are naked.

•

I know I won't be punished if I tell the truth, even if a rule has been broken.

•

I know that no one is allowed to take pictures of my private parts.

•

I have trusted adults I can ask questions of and talk to about my worries.

•

I know what to do if I get separated from my parents in a public place.

•

I follow cyber-safety rules when I'm using the Internet.

•

I know that sexual abuse is never a kid's fault.

•

I know to say "No," try to get away, and tell an adult if anyone tries to touch my private parts.

WE HAVE AN OFF LIMITS HOME!

We regularly talk with our children—no topics are off limits in our home.

•

We do not punish our children for telling the truth about breaking a rule.

•

We listen to and believe our kids.

•

We don't keep secrets in our family.

•

We allow all family members privacy in our home.

•

We are strong enough to handle anything our kids tell us.

•

We do not punish our children regarding their safety.

•

Our children know they do not have to comply with unsafe or inappropriate requests from authority figures.

•

Our kids can choose how they wish to greet people and demonstrate affection.

•

We trust our intuition when it comes to the safety of our children.

•

We carefully screen substitute caregivers.

•

We discuss our children's safety practices with authority figures.

•

We play "What if?" games to promote body-safety skills.

•

We look for teachable moments to reinforce body-safety rules and to discuss sexual development.

•

We know the warning signs of sexual abuse in children and teens.

•

We are informed about sexual abusers and how sexual abuse happens.

•

We understand what makes children and teens vulnerable to sexual abuse.

•

We know how to report suspected child abuse.

•

We have safety rules for using public bathrooms.

•

We have set cyber-safety rules, have protective software on our computers, and monitor our kids' Internet use.

•

When our children spend the night with friends, we regularly check in with them.

•

If our child discloses sexual abuse, we know how to appropriately respond.

•

We know to seek help if we observe sexual types of touching happening with our children.

•

We know the difference between normal sexual curiosity and sexually abusive behaviors.

•

We know how to respond to youths with sexual behavior problems.

WE LIVE IN AN OFF LIMITS COMMUNITY!

We value children and make their safety and well-being a priority.

•

We are aware of the child sexual abuse epidemic and are collectively working to eliminate this major societal problem.

•

We ensure that all youths have access to education in both sexuality and body-safety.

•

We are actively working to eliminate child pornography and the sexualizing of children in the media and advertising.

•

We conduct thorough screening and background checks on all employees and volunteers who have contact with kids.

•

Our schools, youth organizations, and child-care centers have safe-child policies in place.

•

Our children's environments are designed to reduce the likelihood of sexual abuse happening.

•

In our youth organizations, we have policies prohibiting adult-child interactions outside of work-sponsored activities.

•

All employees of children's facilities know how to recognize and report inappropriate behaviors by other staff.

•

We offer training on child sexual abuse to all employees and volunteers in youth-serving organizations.

•

All staff who work with children know the warning signs of sexual abuse and know how to respond to disclosures and how to report suspected abuse.

•

Our medical professionals sensitively screen their patients for the possibility of sexual abuse.

•

We intervene when youths present with signs or symptoms of possible sexual abuse.

•

We provide media campaigns to enhance public awareness of child sexual abuse and educate the public to know that having sex with children is wrong and illegal.

•

We have a social climate that will not tolerate the sexual abuse of children.

•

Our community has specialized treatment providers for victims, families, and abusers.

•

Our community encourages people struggling with sexual thoughts toward children to seek help before sexually abusing a child.

•

We have thoughtful sentencing guidelines and treatment options for people who have sexually abused children.

OFF LIMITS SAFETY TIPS

1. Know the facts about child sexual abusers.
2. Teach children and teens a "safety-in-numbers" rule.
3. Teach young children what to do if they ever become separated from a parent or person in charge.
4. Avoid letting young children go alone into public restrooms.
5. Teach children to always "ask first."
6. Make careful choices about allowing children to be alone with an authority figure.
7. Make sure your children know that they do not have to comply with unsafe or inappropriate requests from an authority figure.
8. Grant all family members the right to privacy.
9. Allow children to choose how they demonstrate affection.
10. Take notice when someone shows lots of attention to one particular child or showers that child with gifts.
11. Actively listen to children.
12. Know the difference between healthy displays of affection and sexual types of touching.
13. Establish a "no-secrets" rule in your home.
14. Know how abusers keep children from telling.
15. Teach children the "Boss of My Body" concept.
16. Teach children body-safety rules.
17. Practice body-safety rules by playing "What if?" games.

18. Take advantage of "teachable moments" to discuss sexual development and body safety.

19. Carefully screen substitute caregivers.

20. Trust your intuition.

21. Be a questioning parent before allowing children to play or sleep at someone else's home.

22. Check in with children when they stay overnight at a friend's home.

23. Be a questioning parent of administrators at your child's school, day care, faith-based institution, and youth-serving organization.

24. Discuss children's safety practices with authority figures.

25. Be a questioning staff member in a school or youth-serving institution.

26. Install protective software on your child's computer.

27. Set cyber-safety rules for children and teens.

28. Know the warning signs of abuse.

29. Help children tell about sexual abuse.

30. Know how to respond to a child's disclosure.

31. Know how to respond to youths with sexual behavior problems.

32. Know how to report suspected sexual abuse.

APPENDIX 2

RESOURCES

Books for Children about Prevention

Federico, J. *Some parts are not for sharing.* Mustang, OK: Tate Publishing and Enterprises, LLC, 2008.

Freeman, L., and C. Deach. *It's my body: A book to teach young children how to resist uncomfortable touch.* Seattle, WA: Parenting Press, 1982.

———. *Loving touches: A book for children about positive, caring kinds of touches.* Seattle, WA: Parenting Press, 1986.

Hammerseng, K. *Telling isn't tattling.* Seattle, WA: Parenting Press, 1995.

Hansen, D. *Those are MY private parts.* Redondo Beach, CA: Empowerment Productions, 2007.

Holsten, J. *The swimsuit lesson: A story for children and parents to enjoy together.* 2nd ed. Fort Collins, CO: Holsten Books, 2006.

Johnsen, K. *The trouble with secrets.* Seattle, WA: Parenting Press, 1986.

Kleven, S. *The right touch: A read-aloud story to help prevent child sexual abuse.* Bellevue, WA: Illumination Arts Publishing Company, 1998.

Sherman, J. *Because it's my body.* Scotch Plains, NJ: S.A.F.E. for Children Publishing, LLC, 2006.

Spelman, C. *Your body belongs to you.* Morton Grove, IL: Albert Whitman & Company, 2000.

Walvoord-Girard, L. *My body is private.* Morton Grove, IL: Albert Whitman & Company, 1984.

Wooden, K. *Child lures: What every parent and child should know about preventing sexual abuse and abduction.* Arlington, TX: The Summit Publishing Group, 1995.

Books for Parents/Professionals about Prevention

Abel, G. *The stop child molestation book: What ordinary people can do in their everyday lives to save 3 million children.* Philadelphia, PA: Xlibris Corporation, 2001.

Baker, L. *Protecting your children from sexual predators.* Darby, PA: Diane Publishing Company, 2002.

De Becker, G. *Protecting the gift: Keeping children and teenagers safe (and parents sane).* New York: The Dial Press Random House, Inc, 1999.

Hammel-Zabin, A. *Conversations with a pedophile: In the interest of our children.* Fort Lee, NJ: Barricade Books, Inc, 2003.

Hart-Rossi, J. *Protect your child from sexual abuse: A parent's guide.* Seattle, WA: Parenting Press, 1984.

Kraizer, S. *The safe child book: A commonsense approach to protecting children and teaching children to protect themselves.* New York: Simon & Shuster, 1985.

Pryor, D. *Unspeakable acts: Why men sexually abuse children.* New York: University Press, 1996.

Salter, A. *Predators, pedophiles, rapists and other sex offenders: Who they are, how they operate, and how we can protect ourselves and our children.* New York: Basic Books, 2003.

Tschirhart-Sandford, L. *The silent children: A book for parents about the prevention of child sexual abuse.* New York: Anchor Books, 1980.

Van Dam, C. *Identifying child molesters: Preventing child sexual abuse by recognizing the patterns of the offenders.* New York: The Haworth Maltreatment and Trauma Press, 2001.

———. *The socially skilled child molester: Differentiating the guilty from the falsely accused.* New York: The Haworth Press, 2006.

Wurtele, S., and C. Miller-Perrin. *Preventing child sexual abuse: Sharing the responsibility.* Lincoln: University of Nebraska Press, 1992.

Materials for Survivors of Sexual Abuse

Adams, J. *The colors within: One rainbow reclaimed.* Philadelphia, PA: Xlibris Corporation, 2006.

Akers, E. *Sarah's Waterfall.* Brandon, VT: The Safer Society Press, 2009.

Bailey Wright, L., and M. Loiselle. *Back on track: Boys dealing with sexual abuse.* Brandon, VT: The Safer Society Press, 1999.

Hindman, J. *A very touching book, for little people and for big people.* Durkee, OR: McClure-Hindman Associates, 1985.

Kehoe, P. *Something happened and I'm scared to tell: A book for young victims of abuse.* Seattle, WA: Parenting Press, 1987.

Ottenweller, J. *Please tell! A child's story about sexual abuse (early steps).* Center City, MN: Hazelden, 1991.

Sanford, D. *I can't talk about it: A child's book about sexual abuse.* Colorado Springs, CO: Multnomah Press, 1986.

Books on Healing and Recovery

Adams, C. *Helping your child recover from sexual abuse.* Seattle, WA: University of Washington Press, 1992.

Bass, E., and L. Davis. *The courage to heal: A guide for women survivors of child sexual abuse.* New York: Harper & Row, 1988.

Bonner, Barbara L., Ph.D. *Taking action: Support for families of adolescents with illegal sexual behavior.* Brandon, VT: Safer Society Press, 2009.

Brady, M. *Daybreak: Meditations for women survivors of sexual abuse.* Center City, MN: Hazelden, 1991.

Brohl, K., and J. Case-Potter. *When your child has been molested: A parents' guide to healing and recovery.* San Francisco, CA: Josey-Bass, 2004.

Feuereisen, P., and C. Pincus. *Invisible girls: The truth about sexual abuse—A book for teen girls, young women, and everyone who cares about them.* Berkeley, CA: Seal Press, 2005.

Gartner, R., and W. Pollack. *Beyond betrayal: Taking charge of your life after boyhood sexual abuse.* Hoboken, NJ: John Wiley & Sons Inc., 2005.

Gil, E. *Outgrowing the pain: A book for and about adults abused as children.* New York: Dell Publishing, 1983.

Mather, C. *How long does it hurt?: A guide to recovering from incest and sexual abuse for teenagers, their friends, and their families.* San Francisco, CA: Josey-Bass, 2004.

Silovsky, Jane F., Ph.D. *Taking action: Support for families of children with sexual behavior problems.* Brandon, VT: Safer Society Press, 2009.

Smith, H. *Fire of the five hearts: A memoir of treating incest.* New York: Taylor & Francis Group, Inc., 2002.

Van Derbur, M. *Miss America by day: Lessons learned from ultimate betrayals and unconditional love.* Colorado: Oak Hill Ridge Press, 2004.

Wiehe, V. *The brother/sister hurt: Recognizing the effects of sibling abuse.* Brandon, VT: The Safer Society Press, 1996.

Sexuality Education Books: Young Children

Brooks, R. and S. Perl. *So that's how I was born.* New York: Simon & Schuster Books for Young Readers, 1983.

Brown, Laura Kransy, and Marc Brown. *What's the big secret?: Talking about sex with girls and boys.* Boston: Little, Brown Young Readers, 2000.

Cavanagh, T. *Understanding children's sexual behaviors: What's natural and healthy.* Oakland, CA: New Harbinger Publications, 1999.

Cole, J. *How you were born.* New York: Harper Collins, 1994.

Eyre, L., and R. Eyre. *How to talk to your child about sex: It's best to start early, but it's never too late—A step-by-step guide for parents.* New York: Golden Guides from St. Martin's Press, 1999.

Gordon, S., and J. Gordon. *Did the sun shine before you were born?* Amherst, NY: Prometheus Books, 1992.

Harris, R. *It's not the stork: A book about girls, boys, babies, bodies, families, and friends.* Massachusetts: Candlewick Press, 2006.

———. *It's so amazing!: A book about eggs, sperm, birth, babies, and families.* Massachusetts: Candlewick Press, 2002.

Mayle, P. *Where did I come from?* New York: Lyle Stuart Books, 2000.

Nilsson, L., and L. Katarina Swanberg. *How was I born?: A child's journey through the miracle of birth.* New York: The Bantam Dell Publishing Group, a division of Random House Inc., 1996.

Richardson, J., and A. Schuster. *Everything you never wanted your kids to know about sex, but were afraid they'd ask: The secrets to surviving your child's sexual development from birth to the teens.* New York: Crown Publishers, a division of Random House Inc., 2003.

Schoen, M. *Bellybuttons are navels.* BookSurge Publishing, 2008.

Schwartz, P., and D. Cappello. *Ten talks parents must have with their children about sex and character.* New York: Hyperion, 2000.

Stinson, K. *The bare-naked book.* Vancouver, BC: Annick Press, 2006.

Sexuality Education Books: Preteens

Cole, J. *Asking about sex and growing up: A question and answer book for boys and girls.* New York: HarperCollins, 1988.

Gitchel, S., and L. Foster. *Let's talk about S-E-X.* Minnetonka, MN: Book Peddlers, 2005.

Harris, R. *It's perfectly normal: changing bodies, growing up, sex, and sexual health.* Massachusetts: Candlewick Press, 2000.

Madaras, L. *The "what's happening to my body?" book for boys.* New York: Newmarket, 2007.

———. *The "what's happening to my body?" book for girls.* New York: Newmarket, 2007.

Madaras, L., and A. Madaras. *What's happening to my body? book for girls; A growing up guide for mothers and daughters.* New York: Newmarket Press, 1984.

Mayle, P. *What's happening to me. Answers to the world's most embarrassing questions.* Secaucus, NJ: L. Stuart, 1975.

Saltz, G. *Changing you: A guide to body changes and sexuality.* New York: Dutton Juvenile, 2007.

Sexuality Education Books: Parents and Teens

Bell Alexander, R., and L. Zeigler-Wildflower. *Talking with your teenager. A book for parents.* New York: Random House Press, 1983.

Calderone, M., and E. Johnson. *Family book about sexuality.* New York: Harper and Row, 1981.

Howard, M. *How to help your teenager postpone sexual involvement.* New York: Continuum Publishing Company, 1988.

Leight, L. *Raising sexually healthy children: A loving guide for parents, teachers, and caregivers.* New York: Rawson Associates, 1988.

Palmer, P. *Teen Esteem.* Toronto: Impact Publishing, 1989.

Sutton, R. *Hearing us out: Voices from the gay and lesbian community.* Toronto: Little Brown and Company, 1997.

Anatomically Detailed Dolls

Amamanta Anatomically Correct Dolls, available at www.amamantafamily.com

Teach-A-Bodies Anatomically Correct Dolls, available at www.teachabodies anatomicaldolls.com

Videos about Childhood Sexuality

What do I say now? 30-minute DVD. Seattle, WA: Committee for Children, 2003. For parents or caregivers of young children, this video addresses setting limits, labeling body parts, how babies are made, self-touch, appropriate/inappropriate touch, and more. http://www.cfchildren.org.

Yes, you can say no. 30-minute DVD. Seattle, WA: Committee for Children, 1988. For parents of preadolescents and adolescents, this video addresses sharing values, keeping communication open, postponing sexual intercourse, avoiding absolutes, building strong relationships, and more. http://www.cfchildren.org.

The growing up series. DVDs. Ottawa, Canada: National Film Board of Canada, 1989. A series of three videos designed for parents to watch with their pre-adolescent children. It serves as an introduction to sexuality education. http://www.tsbvi.edu/Education/sexuality-education-parent.htm.

Raising healthy kids: Families talk about sexual health. DVD. Boston: Health Productions, Inc., 1997. http://www.advocatesforyouth.org.

Where do babies come from? VHS. Concordia Publishing House Family Film, 1988.

Web Sites about Prevention

Child Abuse Prevention Network

child-abuse.com

The Child Abuse Prevention Network is the Internet nerve center for professionals in the field of child abuse and neglect. Child maltreatment, physical abuse, psychological maltreatment, neglect, sexual abuse, and emotional abuse and neglect are key areas of concern, providing unique tools for all workers to support the identification, investigation, treatment, adjudication, and prevention of child abuse and neglect.

Child Molestation Research and Prevention Institute

www.childmolestationprevention.org

A national, science-based nonprofit organization that conducts research to prevent child sexual abuse.

Children Now

www.talkingwithkids.org/about.html

A nonpartisan research and advocacy organization working to raise children's well-being to the top of the national policy agenda.

Committee for Children

www.cfchildren.org

Committee for Children seeks to foster the social and emotional development, safety, and well-being of children through education and advocacy. They develop and publish programs and curricula for children from preschool through middle school about social skills, bullying, and sexual abuse, in addition to an emergent literacy program for young children.

Darkness to Light

www.darknesstolight.org

Their programs raise awareness of the prevalence and consequences of child sexual abuse by educating adults about the steps they can take to prevent, recognize, and react responsibly to the reality of child sexual abuse.

Enough Abuse

www.enoughabuse.org

Provides parents, professionals, and concerned adults with the knowledge and skills needed to prevent child sexual abuse in their homes and communities.

FaithTrust Institute

www.cpsdv.org

FaithTrust Institute is part of the Center for the Prevention of Sexual and Domestic Violence (CPSDV), an international, multifaith organization working to end sexual and domestic violence.

Generation FIVE

www.generationfive.org

Generation FIVE's mission is to end the sexual abuse of children within five generations. Through survivor leadership, community organizing, and public action, Generation FIVE works to interrupt and mend the intergenerational impact of child sexual abuse on individuals, families, and communities.

Guardian of Angels

www.guardianofangels.org

The Guardian of Angels Foundation was created to help reduce the incidence of child sexual abuse through education of child professionals, raising awareness, and educating the public and working with government.

International Center for Assault Prevention

www.internationalcap.org

The mission of the International Center for Assault Prevention (ICAP) is to improve the quality of life for all children worldwide by reducing the level of interpersonal violence against them through the use of primary prevention education and specifically the use of the Child Assault Prevention (CAP) program in their community.

Liberated from Abuse

www.liberatedfromabuse.com

Liberated from Abuse is affiliated with Child Protection and Child Abuse Prevention nonprofit organizations to educate the public on the deviant characteristics of sexual offenders, methods used by pedophiles, and indicators that a child or teen has been abused.

Love Our Children USA

www.loveourchildrenusa.org

Love Our Children USA is a prevention organization for all forms of violence and neglect against children whose commitment is to break the cycle of violence against children.

Miss America By Day

www.MissAmericaByDay.com

Author of *Miss America By Day*, Marilyn Van Derbur offers resources for survivors of sexual abuse as well as resources for sexual abuse prevention and speaking engagements at this Web site.

Mothers Against Sexual Abuse (MASA)

www.againstsexualabuse.org

MASA works to prevent child sexual abuse by increasing adult awareness, connecting victims with resources, and supporting legislation to protect children.

National Children's Advocacy Center (NCAC)

www.nationalcac.org

The National Children's Advocacy Center (NCAC) is a nonprofit organization that provides training, prevention, intervention, and treatment services to fight child abuse and neglect.

National Sexual Violence Resource Center

www.nsvrc.org

The National Sexual Violence Resource Center serves as the nation's principal information and resource center regarding all aspects of sexual violence. It provides national leadership, consultation, and technical assistance by generating and facilitating the development and flow of information on sexual violence intervention and prevention strategies. The NSVRC works to address the causes and impact of sexual violence through collaboration, prevention efforts, and the distribution of resources.

Ophelia's Love

www.opheliaslove.org

Ophelia's Love is an organization that provides information and advocacy as well as survivor and community support through Web-based and community services.

PANdora's Box: The Secrecy of Child Sexual Abuse

www.prevent-abuse-now.com

Provides child protection and abuse prevention information.

Parenting Safe Children, LLC

www.parentingsafechildren.com

Parenting Safe Children is an adult educational workshop where caregivers learn how to keep children safe from sexual abuse and off limits to sexual abusers. Caregivers receive accurate information about child sexual abuse and are provided with actions they can take to prevent children from being sexually abused. Caregivers learn how to modify the home environment so that their family's risk of being chosen by a child molester significantly decreases. Parenting Safe Children workshop schedules are posted on the Web site.

Prevent Child Abuse America (PCAA)

www.preventchildabuse.org

The mission of Prevent Child Abuse America is to "prevent the abuse and neglect of our nation's children" including all forms of abuse and neglect, physical, sexual, educational, and emotional.

Safer Child, Inc.

www.saferchild.org

Provides parents, caregivers, and educators worldwide with the resources and information they need in order to help all children grow up healthy, safe, and happy.

Safer Society Foundation, Inc.

www.safersociety.org

A national resource, research, advocacy, and referral center on the prevention and treatment of sexual abuse.

Stop It Now!

www.stopitnow.com

Stop It Now! prevents the sexual abuse of children by mobilizing adults, families, and communities to take actions that protect children before they are harmed.

Stop the Silence

www.stopcsa.org

The mission of Stop the Silence is to expose and stop child sexual abuse and help survivors heal worldwide.

Vision of Hope

www.theirhope.org

A campaign aimed at protecting children from the devastation of sexual abuse. Vision of Hope promotes research, effective prevention strategies, and adult responsibility and accountability.

Web Sites for Victims and Survivors

Bearing Through It

www.bearingthroughit.org

A Web site dedicated to the journey of healing from childhood sexual abuse.

Child Abuse Prevention Network

child-abuse.com

An Internet center for professionals in the field of child abuse and neglect. The network focuses on child maltreatment, physical abuse, psychological maltreatment, neglect, sexual abuse, and emotional abuse and neglect. It provides tools for all workers to support the identification, investigation, treatment, adjudication, and prevention of child abuse and neglect.

Childhelp USA

www.childhelp.org

Childhelp exists to meet the physical, emotional, educational, and spiritual needs of abused, neglected, and at-risk children. It focuses efforts on advocacy, prevention, treatment, and community outreach.

Childhood Sexual Abuse Survivor Network

www.csasurvivor.net

A Web site for survivors to share and express their thoughts.

Male Survivor

www.malesurvivor.org

Male Survivor is committed to preventing, healing, and eliminating all forms of sexual victimization of boys and men through support, treatment, research, education, advocacy, and activism.

National Center for Missing & Exploited Children

www.missingkids.com

The National Center for Missing & Exploited Children's (NCMEC) mission is to help prevent child abduction and sexual exploitation; help find missing children; and assist victims of child abduction and sexual exploitation, their families, and the professionals who serve them. Includes www.cybertipline.com.

Sibling Abuse Survivors' Information & Advocacy Network (SASIAN)

www.sasian.org

Provides information about the problems associated with sibling sexual abuse.

Stop Educator Sexual Abuse, Misconduct and Exploitation (SESAME)

www.sesamenet.org

SESAME works as a voice for the prevention of sexual exploitation, abuse, and harassment of students by teachers and other school staff.

Survivor Connections, Inc.

www.survivorconnections.net

Promoting activism by survivors of rape, incest, and sexual assault.

Survivors Network of those Abused by Priests

www.snapnetwork.org

SNAP is the nation's largest, oldest and most active support group for women and men wounded by religious authority figures (priests, ministers, bishops, deacons, nuns, and others).

Survivors of Incest Anonymous (SIAWSO)

www.siawso.org

SIA is a 12-step, self-help recovery program modeled after Alcoholics Anonymous. SIA is for men and women, 18 years and older, who were sexually abused as children.

Wings Foundation

www.wingsfound.org

A resource for adult survivors of childhood sexual abuse.

Web Sites with Sex Offender Information

Backgrounds USA

www.backgroundsusa.com

Backgrounds USA is a nationwide employment and background screening company that provides information on public records including criminal records, arrest records, registered sex offenders information, employment histories, tenant checks, and personal references.

Criminal Watch

www.criminalwatch.com

An extensive crime-information portal that features directories for sex offenders, most-wanted criminals, missing kids, deadbeat dads, police departments, attorney generals, and more.

Family Watchdog

www.familywatchdog.us

A free service to locate registered sex offenders in a particular area by simply entering an address.

Kids Need Protection

www.kidsneedprotection.com

A Web site dedicated to catching sex offenders on the Internet.

Map Sex Offenders

www.mapsexoffenders.com

A company offering easy-to-use Web sites that aid users in locating sex offenders in their area.

National Adolescent Perpetration Network (NAPN)

http://www.kempe.org/napn

The NAPN is a cooperative network of multidisciplinary professionals working with sexually abusive youth in the U.S. and abroad with the primary goal of facilitation services for adolescents who are at risk of becoming the next generation of sexual offenders.

STOP Sex Offenders!

www.stopsexoffenders.com

Provides child and family safety information including sex offender registries.

Web Sites about Internet Safety for Kids, Teens, and Parents

www.amw.com/safety/?cat-24

www.besafeonline.org

www.criminaljustice.state.ny.us/missing/i_safety/whatyoushouldknow.htm

www.dmoz.org/Kids_and_Teens/Health/Safety

www.fbi.gov/kids/k5th/safety2.htm

www.internetsafetyforkidsandteens.com

www.internetsuperheroes.org/parents/index.html

www.kids.getnetwise.org

www.netfamilynews.org

www.netsmartz.org

www.pbs.org/parents/growingwithmedia

www.safekids.com

Other Related Web Sites

Association for the Treatment of Sexual Abusers (ATSA)

www.atsa.com

Founded to foster research, facilitate information exchange, and further professional education, and to provide for the advancement of professional standards and practices in the field of sex offender evaluation and treatment. ATSA focuses specifically on the prevention of sexual abuse through effective management of sex offenders.

At Health, Inc.

www.athealth.com/consumer/disorders/self-esteem.html

At Health is a leading provider of mental health information and services for mental health practitioners and those they serve. Its online community consists of psychiatrists, pediatricians, family practitioners, psychologists, psychiatric nurses, social workers, counselors, researchers, educators, school psychologists, caregivers, and others who meet the diverse needs of those with mental health concerns.

Parents, Families and Friends of Lesbians and Gays (PFLAG)

www.pflag.org

PFLAG promotes the health and well-being of gay, lesbian, bisexual, and transgender persons, and their families and friends, through support, skills to cope with an adverse society, and education. PFLAG works to enlighten an ill-informed public, to do advocacy, to end discrimination, and to secure equal civil rights.

Sexuality Education for Children with Visual Impairments: A Parents' Guide

www.tsbvi.edu/Education/sexuality-education-parent.htm

Personal Safety Curricula

This section contains an alphabetical listing of organizations (and individuals) that have created child sexual abuse resources, programs, and/or materials. Each listing provides contact information and a brief description of the resource. For a complete directory of child sexual abuse prevention programs and initiatives, contact the National Sexual Violence Resource Center (www.nsvrc.org) to obtain a copy of *Preventing Child Sexual Abuse: A National Resource Directory and Handbook.*

Body Safety Training (BST)

Sandy Wurtele, founder

www.SandyWurtele.com

Empirically validated personal safety program with workbooks available for parents and for teachers to teach young children (ages three to eight) the knowledge and skills related to preventing childhood sexual abuse. Available in English and Spanish.

Child Abuse Prevention Program (CAPP)

5 Hanover Square, 15th floor, New York, NY 10004; (212) 344-1902

www.childabusepreventionprogram.org

This school-based program's objective is to increase children's sexual abuse prevention knowledge and skills.

Child Advocacy, Resource, and Education, Inc (CARE)

3700 Golden Street, Evans, CO 80620; (970) 356-6751;

www.careweld.org

A school-based prevention program offering children's programs in conjunction with parent-education programs.

FaithTrust Institute

2400 North 45th Street, Suite 101, Seattle, WA 98103; (206) 634-1903

www.faithtrustinstitute.org

An international, multifaith organization working to end sexual and domestic violence. Provides communities and advocates with the tools and knowledge they need to address the religious and cultural issues related to abuse.

Feeling Yes, Feeling No

National Film Board of Canada

P.O. Box 6100, Station Centre-Ville, Montreal, Quebec, H3C 3H5; (800) 283-9000

www.nfb.ca

The Feeling Yes, Feeling No program was developed in 1980 by the Green Thumb Theatre for Young People in Vancouver. The program consists of three instructional 15-minute interactive videos taped by the National Film Board of Canada in 1985. It is available in French as *Mon Corps, C'est Mon Corps.* The videos include children from various ethnic backgrounds, increasing the program's appeal to diverse audiences. The program is often used as part of the personal and social development curriculum whose main objectives are to identify different responses to being touched, to explore reasons why it is hard to tell about "no" feelings, and to teach children how to seek help if touch leaves them feeling "no."

Good Touch/Bad Touch

Childhelp

15757 North 78th Street, Suite B, Scottsdale, AZ 85260; (800) 245-1527

www.childhelp.org.

Objectives are for children to understand the definition of children's sexual abuse and to learn and practice the five basic personal body-safety rules. Children will learn the difference between good, bad, and confusing touch and will learn that no child deserves to be hurt and that abuse is never the child's fault.

International Assault Prevention Project

900 Hollydell Court, Sewell, NJ 08080; (800) 258-3189

www.internationalcap.org

childassaultprevention@gmail.com

The International Center for Assault Prevention is located in Sewell, New Jersey, and is the training center of CAP Projects worldwide. Learn how to become a CAP facilitator, find the nearest CAP project to you, or start one in your area, and, most of all, learn how to keep your children "Safe, Strong, and Free."

No-Go-Tell: Curriculum for Young Children with Special Needs

The James Stanfield Publishing Company, Inc.

P.O. Box 41058, Santa Barbara, CA 93140; (800) 421-6534

www.stanfield.com

The objectives of these programs are increasing recognition and avoidance of sexually threatening and abusive situations, and to teach skills to tell a trusted adult.

Safe Child: Coalition for Children

Sherryll Kraizer, executive director

PO. Box 6304, Denver, CO 80206; (303) 809-9001

Kraizer@safechild.org

www.safechild.org

The objectives include preventing sexual, emotional, and physical abuse of children by familiar people and abuse and abduction by strangers.

SafePlace

P.O. Box 19454, Austin, TX 78760; (512) 267-7233

www.safeplace.org

Provides safety for individuals and families affected by sexual and domestic violence, helps victims in their healing so they can move beyond being defined by the crimes committed against them and become survivors, promotes safe and healthy relationships for the prevention of sexual and domestic violence, and engages the community in advancing alternatives in attitudes, behaviors, and policies to impact our understanding and responses to sexual and domestic violence.

Talking About Touching

Committee for Children

568 First Avenue South, Suite 600, Seattle, WA 98104; (800) 634-4449

clientsupport@cfchildren.org

www.cfchildren.org

The program is intended to increase children's knowledge of and adherence to rules that will help keep them safe, act in assertive ways, and identify differences in safe touch, unsafe touch, and unwanted touch and to follow safety rules about touching.

Touching: A Child Abuse Prevention Program

Community Child Abuse Council of Canada

Hamilton, Ontario, Canada; (905) 523-1020

www.childabusecouncil.on.ca.

Touching is a school-based educational program that includes a DVD plus an accompanying teacher's guide and parent's kit. The program aims to teach and promote child safety with an emphasis on keeping children safe from sexual abuse. The written resources are designed to be used in tandem with the DVD and to facilitate discussion and conversation on the topic.

VIRTUS Online programs

Pat Neal, director

321 South Boston Avenue, Suite 900, Tulsa, OK 74103; (888) 847-8870

www.virtusonline.org

The VIRTUS programs assist religious organizations in being safe havens for children and messengers for preventing child sexual abuse within the church and in society in general. Their child sexual abuse prevention program is Protecting God's Children.

NOTES

Introduction

1. Kofi Annan, in the foreword of *The state of the world's children* 2000 by Carol Bellamy (New York: UNICEF, 2000).

Chapter 1

1. N. Pereda, G. Guilera, M. Forns, and J. Gomez-Benito, "The prevalence of child sexual abuse in community and student samples: A meta-analysis," *Clinical Psychology Review* 29, no. 4 (June 2009): 328–38. Over 100,000 adults from 22 countries were asked about a history of childhood sexual abuse. The analysis showed that 7.9 percent of men and 19.7 percent of women had suffered some form of sexual abuse prior to the age of 18.

2. K. A. Kendall-Tackett, L. M. Williams, and D. Finkehor, "Impact of sexual abuse on children: A review and synthesis of recent empirical studies," *Psychological Bulletin* 113 (1993): 164–80. In a review of empirical studies, up to 40 percent of sexually abused children presented with minor or no clinical symptoms at the time of their evaluation. Also, Susan A. Clancy, *The trauma myth* (New York: Basic Books, 2009). In this groundbreaking and controversial book, author Susan Clancy documents how in most cases of sexual abuse of young children involving nonpenetration, pain, or force, the majority fail to understand the exact nature or meaning of these experiences until some point later in life.

3. Paul Newberry, "Olympic swimming medalist goes public with sexual abuse," *USA Today*, September 16, 2008, http://www.usatoday.com/sports/olympics/2008-09-15-swimming-hoelzer-abuse_N.htm.

4. Margaret Mead, *The world ahead: An anthropologist anticipates the future* (New York: Berghahn Books, 2005).

Chapter 2

1. Douglas W. Pryor, *Unspeakable acts: Why men sexually abuse children* (New York: New York University Press, 1996).

2. Center for Sex Offender Management, "Female sex offenders," Web page. Silver Spring, MD: Center for Sex Offender Management, March 2007, http://www.csom.org/pubs/famale_sex_offenders_brief.pdf (accessed April 26, 2010).

3. Wikipedia contributors, "Mary Kay Letourneau," *Wikipedia, The Free Encyclopedia*, http://en.wikipedia.org/w/index.php?title=Mary_Kay_Letourneau&oldid=355266077 (accessed April 16, 2010).

4. P. A. Fehrenbach and C. Monastersky, "Characteristics of female adolescent sexual offenders," *American Journal of Orthopsychiatry* 58 (1988): 148–51.

5. M. Matlin, *I'll scream later* (New York: Simon Spotlight Entertainment, 2009).

6. T. A. Gannon and M. R. Rose, "Female child sexual offenders: Toward integrating theory and practice," *Aggression and Violent Behavior* 13, no.6 (2008): 422–61.

7. B. E. Saunders, D. G. Kilpatrick, R. F. Hanson, H. S. Resnick, and M. E. Walker, "Prevalence, case characteristics, and long-term psychological correlates of child rape among women: A national survey," *Child Maltreatment* 4 (1999): 187–200; C. Veneziano and L. Veneziano, "Adolescent sex offenders: A review of the literature," *Trauma, Violence & Abuse* 3 (2002): 247–60.

8. Associated Press, "Former MLB player gets 45 years for rape of a minor," *The Herald Dispatch*, June 17, 2009, http://www.herald-dispatch.com/news/briefs/x1227377353/Former-MLB-player-gets-45-years-for-rape-of-minor (accessed April 26, 2010).

9. Javier C. Hernandez, "Stuyvesant Librarian Is Accused of Sexual Abuse," *The New York Times*, June 11, 2009, http://www.nytimes.com/2009/06/12/nyregion/12stuyvesant.html (accessed April 26, 2010).

10. Associated Press, "Frank Lombard, Duke University official, charged in child sex case," *The Huffington Post*, June 27, 2009, http://www.huffingtonpost.com/2009/06/27/frank-lombard-duke-univ-o_n_221900.html (accessed April 26, 2010).

11. Lara Jakes Jordan, "Man accused of raping daughter held in Hong Kong," *The Seattle Times*, May 2, 2007, http://seattletimes.nwsource.com/html/localnews/2003689859_webmolest02m.html (accessed April 26, 2010).

12. Wyatt Haupt, Jr., "Aspen cop, accused of sex crimes and child abuse, resigns," *The Aspen Times*, June 26, 2009, http://www.aspentimes.com/article/20090626/NEWS/906269988&parentprofile=search (accessed April 26, 2010).

13. Nancy Bowman, "Church worker accused of raping girl under 13," *Dayton Daily News*, June 18, 2009, http://www.daytondailynews.com/news/crime/church-worker-accused-of-raping-girl-under-13church-worker-accused-of-raping-girl-under-13-168732.html (accessed April 26, 2010).

14. Kate Williamson, "Child psychiatrist charged with molesting patients," Examiner.com, April 6, 2007, http://www.examiner.com/a-659821~Child_20

psychiatrist_20charged_20with_20molesting_20patients.html (accessed April 26, 2010).

15. P. T. Gustan, "Sex predator-teacher pleads guilty to sex with a student," *Plains Feeder*, July 2, 2008, http://feedlot.blogspot.com/2008/07/ntv-khgikwnbwsws-ca-where-your-news.html (accessed April 26, 2010).

16. Associated Press, "Idaho babysitter accused of having sex with 14-year-old," Foxnews.com, July 9, 2009, http://www.foxnews.com/story/0,2933,530882,00.html (accessed April 26, 2010).

17. Jeremy G. Burton, "Diocese of Scranton priest faces child pornography charges," Standardspeaker.com, October 20, 2009, http://standardspeaker.com/news/diocese-of-scranton-priest-faces-child-pornography-charges-1.348954 (accessed April 26, 2010).

18. Michael Seto, *Pedophilia and sexual offending against children* (Washington, DC: American Psychological Association, 2008).

19. D. A. Simons, S. K. Wurtele, and R. L. Durham, "Developmental experiences of child sexual abusers and rapists," *Child Abuse & Neglect* 32 (2008): 549–60.

20. Local 10 News, "Piano teacher accused of molesting," JustNews.com, April 9, 2008, http://www.justnews.com/news/15829395/detail.html (accessed April 25, 2010).

21. ABC News, "Three More Former Pages Accuse Foley of Online Sexual Approaches," October 5, 2006, http://blogs.abcnews.com/theblotter/2006/10/three_more_form.html (accessed April 26, 2010).

22. Gavin De Becker, *The gift of fear* (Boston: Little, Brown, 1997).

23. The Center for Behavioral Intervention, "Protecting your children: Advice from child molesters," http://www.portlandonline.com/oni/index.cfm?a=244512&c=49723 (accessed April 16, 2010).

Chapter 3

1. J. F. Gilgun and A. Sharma, *Everything you wanted to know about child sexual abuse (or maybe you didn't)* (Morrisville, NC: Lulu Enterprises, 2007).

2. Colorado Department of Corrections, *A guide for parents: Possible indicators of child sexual abuse and things you can do* (Colorado: SOTMP, Colorado Department of Corrections, 1998).

3. M. E. Sprengelmeyer and K. Vaughan, "Stalking children: Imprisoned molesters reveal dark secrets, tell Colorado's parents how to protect their children," *Rocky Mountain News* 5a (October 8, 2000): 41–5a.

4. M. Elliott, K. Browne, and J. Kilcoyne, "Child sexual abuse prevention: What offenders tell us," *Child Abuse & Neglect* 19 (1995): 579–94.

5. C. van Dam, *Identifying child molesters by recognizing the patterns of the offenders* (Binghamton, NY: The Haworth Press, Inc., 2001).

6. W. E. Prendergast, *Sexual abuse of children and adolescents: A preventive guide for parents, teachers, and counselors* (New York: Continuum, 1996).

7. Jace Larson, "Molester warns parents: 'Kids are always interested,'" 9News.com, October 30, 2008, http://www.9news.com/news/article.aspx?storyid=102887&catid=339 (accessed April 26, 2010).

8. S. Angel, "Don't be afraid to say 'No!'" *Redbook* (July 1978): 40.

9. This was a T-shirt that was part of the Clothesline Project, begun in 1990 when members of the Cape Cod Women's Agenda hung a clothesline across the village green in Hyannis, Massachussetts, with 31 shirts designed by survivors of assult, rape, and incest. Since the first display, the Clothesline Project has had an estimated 35,000 shirts added to the display.

10. L. T. Sanford, *The silent children: A parent's guide to the prevention of child sexual abuse* (New York: Doubleday, 1980).

Chapter 4

1. A. Hammel-Zabin, *Conversations with a pedophile* (New York: Newmarket Press, 2003).

2. L. Berliner and J. R. Conte, "The process of victimization: The victims' perspective," *Child Abuse & Neglect* 14 (1990): 29–40.

3. Douglas W. Pryor, *Unspeakable acts: Why men sexually abuse children* (New York: New York University Press, 1996).

4. Berliner and Conte, "The process of victimization."

5. C. van Dam, *Identifying child molesters by recognizing the patterns of the offenders* (Binghamton, NY: The Haworth Press, Inc., 2001).

6. Berliner and Conte, "The process of victimization."

7. Berliner and Conte, "The process of victimization."

8. L. T. Sanford, *The silent children: A parent's guide to the prevention of child sexual abuse* (New York: Doubleday, 1980).

Chapter 5

1. A. Hammel-Zabin, *Conversations with a pedophile* (New York: Newmarket Press, 2003).

2. Douglas W. Pryor, *Unspeakable acts: Why men sexually abuse children* (New York: New York University Press, 1996).

3. M. Van Derbur, *Miss America by day* (Denver, CO: Oak Hill Ridge Press, 2004).

4. D. W. Smith, E. J. Letourneau, B. E. Saunders, D. G. Kilpatrick, H. S. Resnick, and C. L. Best, "Delay in disclosure of childhood rape: Results from a national study," *Child Abuse & Neglect* 24, no. 2 (2000): 273–87.

5. Associated Press, "Letter to Santa leads to sex abuse charges," CBS News, December 16, 2008, http://www.cbsnews.com/stories/2008/12/16/national/main4670951.shtml (accessed April 26, 2010).

6. L. A. Fontes, "Sin Vergüenza: Addressing shame with Latino victims of child sexual abuse and their families," *Journal of Child Sexual Abuse* 16 (2007): 61–83.

7. Pryor, *Unspeakable acts.*

Chapter 6

1. S. K. Wurtele, and C. L. Miller-Perrin, *Preventing child sexual abuse: Sharing the responsibility* (Lincoln: University of Nebraska Press, 1992).

2. D. W. Haffner, *From diapers to dating*, 2nd ed. (New York: Newmarket Press, 2004).

3. D. Satcher, *The Surgeon General's call to action to promote sexual health and responsible sexual behavior* (Washington, DC: U.S. Department of Health and Human Services, 2001).

4. W. D. Mosher, A. Chandra, and J. Jones, "Sexual behavior and selected health measures: Men and women 15–44 years of age, United States, 2002," *Vital and Health Statistics* 362 (2005): 1–56; L. D. Lindberg, R. Jones, and J. S. Santelli, "Noncoital sexual activities among adolescents," *Journal of Adolescent Health* 43 (2008): 231–38.

5. M. E. Sprengelmeyer and K. Vaughan, "Stalking children: Imprisoned molesters reveal dark secrets, tell Colorado's parents how to protect their children," *Rocky Mountain News* 5a (October 8, 2000): 41–5a.

6. S. K. Wurtele, *The body-safety training workbook* (Colorado Springs, CO: self-published, 2007).

7. Wurtele, *The body-safety training workbook.*

8. L. Berliner and J. R. Conte, "The process of victimization: The victims' perspective," *Child Abuse & Neglect* 14 (1990): 29–40.

9. Wurtele, *The body-safety training workbook.*

10. L. Baker, *Protecting your children from sexual predators* (New York: St. Martin's Press, 2002).

11. S. K. Wurtele and J. S. Owens, "Teaching personal safety skills to young children: An investigation of age and gender across five studies," *Child Abuse & Neglect* 21 (1997): 805–14.

12. C. van Dam, *Identifying child molesters by recognizing the patterns of the offenders* (Binghamton, NY: The Haworth Press, Inc., 2001).

13. J. R. Conte, S. Wolf, and T. Smith, "What sexual offenders tell us about prevention strategies," *Child Abuse & Neglect* 13 (1989): 293–301; M. Elliott, K. Browne, and J. Kilcoyne, "Child sexual abuse prevention: What offenders tell us," *Child Abuse & Neglect* 19 (1995): 579–94; Sprengelmeyer and Vaughan, "Stalking children."

Chapter 7

1. Gavin De Becker, *The gift of fear* (Boston: Little, Brown, 1997).

2. R. Shoop, *Sexual exploitation in schools: How to spot it and stop it* (Thousand Oaks, CA: Corwin Press, 2003).

3. D. Finkelhor and L. M. Williams, *Nursery crimes: Sexual abuse in day care* (New York: Guilford, 1998).

4. John Jay College, "Nature and Scope of Sexual Abuse of Minors by Catholic Priests and Deans in the United States, 1950–2002" available at http://www.jjay.cuny.edu/churchstudy/.

5. Sandra G. Boodman, "How deep the scars of abuse?" *The Washington Post,* July 29, 2002, http://www.snapnetwork.org/psych_effects/how_deep_scars.htm (accessed April 25, 2010).

6. D. Finkelhor, *Childhood victimization: Violence, crime, and abuse in the lives of young people* (New York: Oxford University Press, Inc., 2008).

Chapter 8

1. S. C. Dombrowski, K. L. Gischlar, and T. Durst, "Safeguarding young people from cyber pornography and cyber sexual predation: A major dilemma of the Internet," *Child Abuse Review* 16 (2007): 153–70.

2. Walecia Konrad, "It's 2007: Do you know where your kids are?" *Good Housekeeping,* www.goodhousekeeping.com/kids-monitoring-technology-mar07 (accessed April 25, 2010).

3. Wendy Lazarus and Laurie Lipper, *Parents' guide to the information superhighway: Rules and tools for families online* (The Children's Partnership, May 1998), available for download at http://www.childrenspartnership.org/AM/Template.cfm?Section=Home&CONTENTID=4687&TEMPLATE=/CM/HTMLDisplay.cfm (accessed April 26, 2010).

4. J. Wolak, K. J. Mitchell, and D. Finkelhor, *Online victimization of youth: Five years later* (Alexandra, VA: National Center for Missing & Exploited Children, 2006), available at http://www.unh.edu/ccrc/pdf/CV138.pdf (accessed April 26, 2010).

5. L. A. Malesky, Jr., "Predatory online behavior: Modus operandi of convicted sex offenders in identifying potential victims and contacting minors over the Internet," *Journal of Child Sexual Abuse* 16 (2007): 23–32.

6. J. Wolak, D. Finkelhor, and K. Mitchell, "Internet-initiated sex crimes against minors: Implications for prevention, based on findings from a national study," *Journal of Adolescent Health* 35 (2004): 424.e11–424e20.

7. K. Eichenwald, "Through his Web cam, a boy joins a sordid online world," *The New York Times,* December 19, 2005.

8. "Victims parents want action against online predators," ABC News.com, August 4, 2007, http://abcnews.go.com/WN/Technology/story?id=3447710&page=1 (accessed April 26, 2010).

9. Local 10 News, "Police: Man molested girl he lured on MySpace," JustNews.com, April 30, 2008, http://www.justnews.com/news/16083232/detail.html?rss=mia&psp=news (accessed April 26, 2010).

10. Nicole Weisensee Egan, "Abducted, enslaved—and now, talking about it," *People Magazine* 67, no. 15 (April 16, 2007), available at http://www.people.com/people/archive/article/0,,20061919,00.html (accessed April 26, 2010).

11. J. Wolak, D. Finkelhor, K. J. Mitchell, and M. L. Ybarra, "Online 'predators' and their victims: Myths, realities, and implications for prevention and treatment," *American Psychologist* 63, no. 2 (2008): 111–28.

Chapter 9

1. S. K. Wurtele and C. L. Miller-Perrin, *Preventing child sexual abuse: Sharing the responsibility* (Lincoln: University of Nebraska Press, 1992).

2. M. Van Derbur, *Miss America by day* (Denver, CO: Oak Hill Ridge Press, 2004).

3. R. K. Oates, D. P. H. Jones, D. Denson, A. Sirotnak, N. Gary, and R. D. Krugman, "Erroneous concerns about child sexual abuse," *Child Sexual Abuse* 24, no. 1 (2000): 149–57.

4. L. A. Fontes, "Sin Vergüenza: Addressing shame with Latino victims of child sexual abuse and their families," *Journal of Child Sexual Abuse* 16 (2007): 61–83.

5. Mary Tyler Moore, *After all* (New York: Putnam, 1995).

6. G. Ryan, "Childhood sexuality: A decade of study. Part I—Research and curriculum development," *Child Abuse & Neglect* 24 (2000): 33–48.

7. T. Cavanagh-Johnson, "Child perpetrators—children who molest other children: Preliminary findings," *Child Abuse & Neglect* 12 (1988): 219–29; Ryan, "Childhood sexuality."

8. K. B. Hagans and J. Case, *When your child has been molested* (Lexington, MA: Lexington Books, 1988).

Epilogue

1. D. Finkelhor, *Childhood victimization: Violence, crime, and abuse in the lives of young people* (New York: Oxford University Press, Inc., 2008).

2. Mahatma Gandhi, as quoted in "Arun Gandhi shares the Mahatma's message" by Michel W. Potts, in *India-West* (San Leandro, California), vol. 27, no. 13 (February 1, 2002), p. A34; Arun Gandhi indirectly quoting his grandfather.

ABOUT THE AUTHORS

SANDY K. WURTELE, Ph.D., is a psychologist and professor in the department of psychology at the University of Colorado at Colorado Springs. She currently directs the undergraduate program and chairs the Institutional Review Board for Human Subjects. She has been studying childhood sexual abuse (CSA) since 1986 and is recognized as an international expert in CSA prevention. Dr. Wurtele is the author of educational and scholarly materials for professionals, parents, and children. She is a popular conference speaker and workshop facilitator for professionals and parents.

FEATHER BERKOWER, M.S.W., is a 25-year veteran in child sexual abuse prevention. Using a community-oriented approach, she has trained over 70,000 school children and 35,000 parents. Her well-regarded workshop, Parenting Safe Children, empowers adults to keep children safe from sexual abuse. She presents in homes, schools, youth organizations, parenting groups, and businesses. Before founding Parenting Safe Children, Berkower was co-director for a regional chapter of the Child Assault Prevention Program, which delivers school-based curricula that helps keep children and teens safe from bullying and sexual assault. Berkower is a licensed clinical social worker and holds a master's of social welfare from the University of California, Berkeley. She conducts media interviews, workshops, and private consultations throughout the United States regarding issues of child safety and child sexual assault prevention. Berkower lives in Colorado with her husband.

INDEX